M000087814

Arizona Wine

Arizona Wine

A HISTORY OF PERSEVERANCE & PASSION

CHRISTINA BARRUETA

Foreword by Chef Mark Tarbell

AMERICAN PALATE

Published by American Palate
A Division of The History Press
Charleston, SC
www.historypress.com

Copyright © 2019 by Christina Barrueta
All rights reserved

Front cover, top, left to right: The Carlson men harvest at sunrise. *Jenelle Bonifield, courtesy of Carlson Creek Vineyard*; Wine grapes. *Callaghan Vineyards*; Waverly Brown pours her family's Callaghan wine at the Arizona Wine Collective. *Author's photo*; *bottom*: Coronado Vineyards in Willcox. *Michelle Jonas.*
Back cover, top: Page Springs Cellars. *Grace Stufkosky, courtesy of Page Springs Cellars*; *bottom*: Young Sagrantino vines at Sand-Reckoner Vineyards. *Michell Jonas.*

First published 2019

Manufactured in the United States

ISBN 9781467140843

Library of Congress Control Number: 2019943523

Notice: The information in this book is true and complete to the best of our knowledge. It is offered without guarantee on the part of the author or The History Press. The author and The History Press disclaim all liability in connection with the use of this book.

All rights reserved. No part of this book may be reproduced or transmitted in any form whatsoever without prior written permission from the publisher except in the case of brief quotations embodied in critical articles and reviews.

To my husband, Ernesto, who is eternally encouraging and unfailingly supportive of all my endeavors.

Contents

Contents

Foreword

If I had been asked who might best write Arizona's wine history, Christina would have been at the top of the list. A longtime proponent and promoter of the food and wine culture in Arizona, she has documented through her writings and prolific social media presence the renaissance that's quietly changed our state over the last few decades.

This book is the culmination of years of travel throughout Arizona, of relationships with the hardworking winemakers whose challenges and triumphs she has witnessed firsthand and of meticulous research into the past. Although there had been winemaking here for years, it wasn't generally recognized and certainly not appreciated. I remember that seminal moment when Kent Callaghan grabbed some national attention from Robert Parker in 1994. Before this, Arizona wine was considered a joke; people thought of us as a desolate terrain hostile to vines. There was no understanding at all of the multifaceted climates and soils we have to work with. It took smart, tenacious and dedicated winemakers to look specifically at those facets and figure out what they could do with them. Just as California started as one giant wine state and slowly divided into the complicated regions and subregions that now define it, Arizona has been carving out the identity of its own regions that represent an enormous variety. Our passionate and daredevil vignerons are doing amazing things with Malvasia, Tempranillo, Grenache, Syrah, Viognier and Nebbiolo (to name but a few).

My passion for wine started as a culinary student in Paris in the early '80s when, for a hobby, I attended l'Academie du Vin. This experience ignited my passion for wine, which, combined with my love of food and hospitality, has made for a wonderful journey. I have tasted Arizona wine with growing interest since moving to the state in 1986. Watching the development of Arizona winemaking has been fascinating, and I'm so excited about our state's wine industry. I'm confident in stating that it will be different than any other wine-growing state in our country. As a longtime champion of all things local, I couldn't be happier to see the history and the future of Arizona wine captured by "one of our own" in Christina's tribute to what perseverance and passion can attain.

—Mark Tarbell, chef and restaurateur

Acknowledgements

I'm grateful for my loving family and for my husband, Ernesto, who supported me in the many hours I devoted to researching this book and sampling the vintners' wares. I would also like to thank Rhonni and Josh Moffitt, who invited me more than a decade ago to write for their just-launched magazine, *Arizona Vines & Wines*, which introduced me to the wonderful world of Arizona wine and the inspiring people behind it. Finally, a heartfelt thank-you to the passionate winemakers and winegrowers who welcomed me into their homes, their businesses and their lives. I hope I have shared your voices of passion and determination in a way that did you justice.

Chapter 1

The Vineyards of Arizona

In the high-elevation grasslands of Sonoita and Elgin, pronghorn antelope roam and cattle graze. An hour's drive brings you to the Willcox basin in southeastern Arizona surrounded by the picturesque ranges of Dos Cabezas, Dragoon and Chiricahua Mountains. Head north to the highlands of central Arizona and you'll find yourself in the lush canyons of Verde Valley fed by the Verde River.

What these three distinct Arizona regions have in common is wine—award-winning wine.

Unbeknownst and still a surprise to many, a confluence of factors contributes to Arizona's rise as a rapidly maturing winegrowing region, bringing in $56.2 million in wine tourism in 2017, according to a study by the Arizona Office of Tourism. Traversing the varied topographical regions of the state, scenic tasting rooms can be found perched on mountainsides with majestic valley panoramas, nestled alongside burbling creeks underneath the dappled shade of desert oak trees or set on grassland plateaus with sweeping views of desert plains and rocky peaks.

Visitors will discover over one hundred bonded wineries producing a diverse range of wines, from Cabernet Sauvignon and Chardonnay to Tannat and Malvasia Bianca. "We have great photosynthesis, a nice dry climate and good elevation," says Michael Pierce, winemaker at Bodega Pierce and director of enology at the Southwest Wine Center at Yavapai College. "We have all the aspects to grow wine grapes, so the list of varieties that do well in Arizona is very long. The list that don't do well is pretty short, which, as a winemaker, is exciting."

The view from Rune Wines tasting room in Sonoita. *Author's collection.*

ARIZONA'S WINE REGIONS

Sonoita, located approximately fifty miles south of Tucson in southeastern Arizona, lays claim to receiving Arizona's first designation as an American Viticultural Area (AVA) in 1984. Initial inhabitants were Native Americans, and over the centuries, Spanish explorers and Jesuit priests who may have planted Mission grapes arrived, along with miners and cattle ranchers who settled in the area with the building of the Santa Fe Railroad. Here, in the 1970s, soil scientist Dr. Gordon Dutt founded the modern-day winemaking era, paving the way for Arizona's now-thriving industry. At an elevation of five thousand feet, Arizona's first AVA is currently home to over fifteen tasting rooms and wineries.

Nearby Willcox received its AVA title in 2016 and has continued to flourish, now producing approximately 75 percent of the grapes grown in the Grand Canyon State. Boasting alluvial deposits, volcanic soil and an elevation to 4,500 feet, the vineyards of the Willcox Bench are turning out some of the most awarded wines made in Arizona. Circumscribing a 526,000-acre area within Graham and Cochise Counties, the basin is a large valley surrounded by striking mountain ranges with more than a dozen tasting rooms drawing visitors to this expanding wine region.

In the heart of Arizona lies the Verde Valley, a 714-square-mile area that encompasses the towns of Camp Verde, Cottonwood, Jerome, Sedona and Cornville. Close to 80 percent of the land is National Forest, including Coconino National Forest, home to the famous red rocks of Sedona. It possesses a divergent landscape where you'll find aspen trees and bristlecone pine in the higher elevations and desert willow and barrel cactus in the lower elevations. The Verde River runs through this beautiful valley defined by Mingus Mountain and Mogollon Rim, and the region's limestone and volcanic soils support over twenty-five tasting rooms and wineries.

Climatic variances have the most impact on wine grape production, and Arizona's higher elevations with warm days and cool nights create a sought-after dramatic swing in temperature. The diurnal temperature range, or the difference between highs and lows in a twenty-four-hour period, affects the grape's ripening process and balance of sugar and acidity. "What you're looking for," explains Curt Dunham of LDV Winery, "is that thirty-degree-plus diurnal temperature difference between the daytime high and the nighttime low. That's the common denominator of all fine wine grapes, that temperature swing, which Arizona has because of the altitude of the vineyards." This diurnal shift is affected by bodies of water (such as California wine country and Pacific Ocean maritime patterns), humidity, wind and elevation, and the semi-arid high-elevation vineyards of Arizona, though they have drawn comparison to celebrated wine regions of Spain, Argentina and France, are uniquely their own. In his article "Geography and Strong Wines" in *AZ Wine Lifestyle*, Mark Beres, co-founder of Flying Leap Vineyards, commented on the growing conditions found in Arizona:

> *Our geographical location gives Arizona grape farmers long growing seasons, full sun and bountiful fruit yields of grapes high in sugar and, in the case of red grapes, deeply-colored skins, producing many exceptional wines of relatively high alcohol content and impressive body, color depth and structure. Additionally, our long growing season spreads out our harvest activities considerably, which gives farm wineries here great latitude in harvest timing and helps with the logistics of bringing in the fruit and processing the harvest into wine at the winery.*

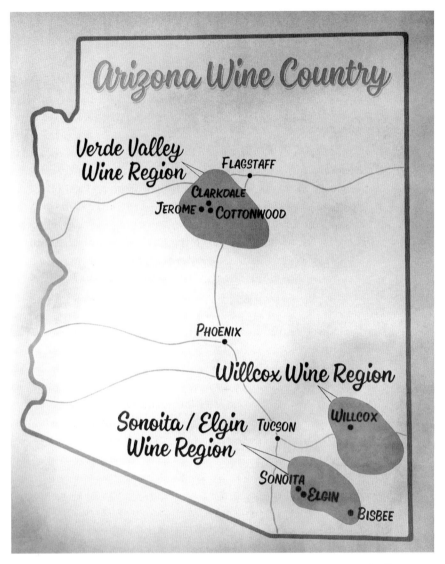

A map of Arizona's wine regions at the Arizona Wine Collective tasting room in Tucson. *Author's collection.*

WINE INDUSTRY CHALLENGES

But growing grapes in a burgeoning wine region is fraught with challenges too. Contrary to what some may surmise, heat and arid conditions aren't the most problematic issue with Arizona grape growing; more detrimental is cold and excessive rain. "There's the assumption that all of Arizona looks like Phoenix, and so people have a hard time fathoming that you can grow good grapes," says Todd Bostock of Dos Cabezas WineWorks. "Or that it's too hot here, which is interesting, since most of the issues we run into are cold and wet-related." Late-spring frosts damage young green shoots, and hail can decimate acres of vines. In his article "Frost in Arizona—What the Rest of the Country Doesn't Know" for *AZ Wine Lifestyle*, Eric Glomski of Page Springs Cellars writes of the vintage of 2009, when he lost an estimated seventy tons of grapes to an April freeze. Kief Manning of Kief-Joshua Vineyards has shared with *Wines Vines Analytics* about losing 90 percent of his crop in a 2010 hailstorm. Arizona's annual monsoons, with wind shifts that bring in tropical moisture from the Gulfs of California and Mexico, can wreak the most havoc, as these wet conditions often coincide with late-summer harvests.

"I don't think the challenge with monsoons can be overstated," says Kent Callaghan of Callaghan Vineyards. "It's completely different, for example, from the West Coast, where they're dry in the summer and get winter rain. Tropical moisture is the worst. It depends on how much rainfall, how it falls and if you get dry periods in between," he explains. "In 2013 and 2014, we had the same amount of rainfall, but in '13, we had dry periods nicely spaced between heavy rain, and it was a big vintage in terms of volume and fruit. But 2014? Total nightmare. We had between fourteen and sixteen days where it rained or it was so humid that the vines never dried out and the soil stayed wet. There was no wind, no movement of air. It was crazy. I had never seen Cabernet rot, and I lost all the Tempranillo because at that point there's nothing you can really do to ameliorate things. We had the same amount of rain, but it mattered how it fell."

For tenacious Arizona pioneers in a nascent wine-growing region, adjusting to these challenges requires resilience and a philosophical approach to learn from losses and determine which grapes perform the best in certain conditions. On the other hand, for a new wine-growing region that has not yet defined itself, experimentation and trial and error can be the inspiration for spectacular wines. "In understanding the struggles," shares Maynard Keenan of Caduceus Cellars, "I've talked to a lot of winemakers

Since grapes are dormant in winter, they suffer little damage from the snow. *Pillsbury Wine Company.*

and found that the grapes that grew right on that edge between success and failure—that frictional edge—produce some of the best wines." Sommelier James Monaci, wine columnist and founder of Monaci Enoteca, agrees. "One of the acknowledged philosophies of wine production and farming is that stressed grapes produce better wine due to the concentration of juice and complexity," he says. "Take, for example, Spain, where they grow Tempranillo. The vines are grown in gravelly and rocky soils where the roots have to go deep to get water to survive. They're being stressed, but the wine is remarkable."

The Arizona wine industry also must battle misconceptions of dusty grapevines grown among cacti in blazing sun. "Whenever I've spoken to people outside the state or outside the country about Arizona, they think of Phoenix as concrete and cactus," says Robert Carlson of Carlson Creek Vineyard. "They don't realize that a major part of the state is at elevation and that we have the largest stand of Ponderosa pines in the world." "People don't realize the diversity of Arizona," agrees Peggy Fiandaca of LDV Winery, "so it's a perception that we struggle with. People don't understand us; they don't understand the state."

Another hurdle Arizona is working to overcome is the preconceived notion of inexpensive, low-quality wine. For some, their initial introduction may have been souvenir or novelty labels, while others have an expectation of wine produced in Arizona equating to bargain bottles. Consumers more familiar with the price point of mass-produced wines can be surprised that Arizona's small-batch wines are not cheap. "If you want a five-dollar wine," says Sam Pillsbury of Pillsbury Wine Company, "you have to do it in massive amounts with massive everything. Harvesting, picking, making it mechanically and fifty-thousand-gallon tanks. You don't barrel ferment everything and pick stuff by hand like we do. You can't."

"It's different here," Pillsbury continues. "My great-great-grandfather didn't plant the vineyard. It costs a lot of money to build a new infrastructure, and then you have to maintain that vineyard for years. You can't even produce a significant crop for five years off of that. So you make wine from the five-year-old crop, and if it's a red, it's two years in a barrel. Then you bottle it, and then it's in a bottle for another year and then you sell it. You're looking at more than a decade for the start, so it will be more expensive than that mass-produced wine, but it should help people appreciate why Arizona wine isn't cheap."

The varied topography of Arizona includes grapevines and rosebushes. *Rhonni Moffitt.*

Slowly but surely, however, the tide has begun to turn. As more consumers explore what is being coaxed out of the Grand Canyon State, Arizona's wines are being recognized and appreciated, and the nation is starting to take notice. In 2019, Pillsbury entered fourteen wines and took home fourteen medals from the prestigious San Francisco Chronicle Wine Competition, including a Best in Class for his Malvasia Bianca and a fourth Double Gold for his WildChild White. Many other hardworking winemakers likewise have been bringing home medals and accolades, proving that award-winning, world-class wines can, and are, being made in Arizona. As Eric Glomski commented in *Frontdoors Media* after two Arizona wines—his Page Springs Cellars and Corey Turnbull's and Mitch Levy's Burning Tree Cellars—were recognized with ninety-point scores by *Wine Spectator* in 2013:

> *We've been dealt our share of challenges as winegrowers in Arizona— both in the uncharacteristically unique trials of the land and climate, to overcoming and winning over perceptions of Arizona as a winemaking region at all....We're so proud of the wine industry here in Arizona, and are more than thrilled to be producing the caliber of wines that we always knew was possible.*

This fortitude and determination is the hallmark of Arizona's band of passionate vignerons, a pioneering optimism and unifying spirit that spans generations both past and present.

Chapter 2

Southern Arizona's Early History

THE SPANISH COLONIAL ERA

It is well documented that wine cultivation in the Americas traces its origins to Mexico, home to the oldest vineyards, with the arrival of the Spanish in the sixteenth century. Bringing along winemaking traditions and introducing European wine grapes (*Vitis vinifera*), they had much success with a variety confirmed in 2007 by DNA analysis to be Listán Prieto, or what we know as the Mission grape, a name derived from its association with mission vineyards and sacramental wine. Its expansion north reached Texas and New Mexico around 1630, and San Franciscan monks are credited with introducing the Mission grape in the late eighteenth century to California, but when it made its way across the modern-day border to Arizona is a bit murkier.

Some claim that Jesuit priests were making wines in Arizona missions a century before California, but it's a premise that writer and Southwest historian Erik Berg has found difficult to verify. "While Mission grapes did dominate on the Spanish frontier, I have found no historic accounts of missionaries making wine in Arizona during the Spanish period," he notes. "There's circumstantial evidence that wine was probably made toward the very end of the Spanish period, but most likely not before the late 1700s.

"I originally went in thinking there would be some Spanish winemaking, and I just wanted to find the earliest firsthand Spanish accounts," he says. With prior expertise in the territorial era, Berg has found himself delving

Vineyard grapes. *Becky Limberg.*

into the Spanish colonial period, spending the last three years researching and authenticating a comprehensive history. "Wine has always been a part of Arizona history," he emphasizes. "During the territorial period, wine was every bit as popular as beer and whiskey, and even during Prohibition, people were making their own wine at home. Wine has had a long history. Many of the people that immigrated here were from wine-drinking cultures, and so wine has been a part of Arizona history from the time the first Europeans arrived. It's been an important part of the culture and the economy, and I think its history has been overlooked."

He expounds further in his 2018 article "Equal Age for Age: The Growth, Death, and Rebirth of an Arizona Wine Industry, 1700–2000" in the *Journal of Arizona History*:

> *Arizona's wine history is surprisingly rich and well aged—the current iteration being just the latest budding of an ancient vine with roots that long predate the state, and probably even the territory. Its earliest origins are the subject of legends and misconceptions stemming from the fading twilight of the Spanish colonial empire. It evolved in the pioneering days of the Arizona territory and helped inspire the agricultural revolution that would transform the Salt River Valley.*

Berg addresses the growth of viticulture in the Spanish colonial Southwest, noting that successful mission-era vineyards in Arizona are sparse or even nonexistent in the documentation he has uncovered thus far. He lists factors such as many missions being located in regions not conducive to winegrowing; it taking years for a new vineyard to produce a significant amount of fruit for winemaking; and the few mission priests who had the time and expertise to cultivate, produce and store the results of their harvest. Another erroneous assumption, according to Berg in his article, was the large amount of sacramental wine needed at the missions.

> *But the congregation sharing wine is a relatively recent practice, only becoming widespread in the last century. During the mission period, the Catholic Church followed the precepts of the older Tridentine Mass and only the priests took wine. As a result, the early missions and churches required only a modest store of sacramental wine for religious purpose. In much of the Southwest, this wine was sent to the missions from major supply centers along with other critical items like lamp and holy oil, candle wax, and writing paper.*

Historical anecdotes frequently point to Father Eusebio Francisco Kino, the legendary explorer and Jesuit priest who successfully established twenty-four missions across Pimería Alta, the borderlands of today's regions of southern Arizona and northern Sonora, Mexico. This included the famous Mission Nuestra Señora de los Dolores in Sonora. As documented in a translation of *Kino's Historical Memoir of Pimería Alta: A Contemporary Account of the Beginnings of California, Sonora, and Arizona*, here is where, in a 1705 *informe*, he described "very good orchards and vineyards to make wine for the masses." Señora de los Dolores served as a home base while the padre visited villages in Arizona to establish other missions. Berg, however, raises questions about the existence of grape-bearing vineyards in these locations, citing the fact that documents show that many of the Arizona missions "were in name only" and did not house resident priests or staff. As Berg observed:

> *The brief exception was in 1701, when Kino did assign a pair of priests to Guevavi [Nogales] and San Xavier Del Bac [Tucson] but both soon left their post due to illness. If the priests had attempted to plant grape vines, they certainly did not stay long enough to ensure they would mature and bear fruit.*

Mission San Xavier del Bac in Tucson. *Brian J. Zahn.*

It's not until the end of the Spanish colonial period in the late 1700s that reports of grape-growing in regions around Tucson and Tubac make an appearance, leading to the assumption that winemaking may have also been taking place at this time. Rather than reports of the abundance of wine in the 1700s, however, history shows a scarcity. In 1757, Father Bernard Middendorff at San Agustin near Tucson bemoaned the lack of wine for Mass, and in 1787, an inventory at Xavier del Bac lists fields of grain and a vegetable garden but no mention of a vineyard and just four jugs of wine in the storeroom.

As Berg notes in his article, Father Ignacio Pfefferkorn, who served the area for over a decade starting in 1756, asserted that winemaking attempts in the region had proven to be a "fruitless undertaking" due both to a lack of expertise and "because it rains there daily in July and August when the grapes must ripen and hence they would either rot or would not mature."

"There is a tiny window back in the early 1600s up in Awatovi [northeastern Arizona] where the Spanish were there long enough for grape vines to take root," Berg admits, "but it's a bad growing place at 6,000 feet and there's no historical or archeological evidence of this. It's not impossible, but it's very unlikely. My experience in researching the larger Southwest is that missionaries, being the first people to enter an area, would sometimes plant grapes if they were in a good spot, but it was generally the settlers that came along later who had an economic interest in making wine." Berg writes:

But the larger historical record clearly indicates that, with the exception of El Paso, missionary winemaking in the Southwest—and particularly in Arizona—was not as common and widespread as often believed. Instead, wine production in the region centered around a few locations and was probably the work of local Spanish settlers as often as mission priests.

THE TERRITORIAL SOUTHWEST

The earliest mentions of successful grape vineyards in southern Arizona begin appearing in the 1800s. In 1867, J.W. "Jack" Swilling formed the Swilling Irrigating and Canal Company to claim water from the Salt River, completing his ambitious irrigation project in 1868. Within a year, the community's members were cultivating hundreds of acres of farmland in what they called the Phoenix settlement, including table grapes. A writer in an 1870 letter to the *Prescott Miner* shared:

> *A few grape vines were planted here two years ago, and as those who did it had no confidence in their production, they were uncared for; but this season Messrs. Swilling and Starar each had a fine crop of as delicious grapes as ever grew in California, and they, as well as others, have determined to henceforth plant and properly cultivate vineyards.*

By 1872, wine grapes were documented as being grown in the Salt River Valley, mainly around the town of Mesa, though, once again, farmers faced challenges such as monsoon rain rot, summer heat and California wine competition.

"Who actually had the first winery in the Salt River Valley," says Berg, "is hard to say. If a name had to be put to it, it would probably be Daniel and Samuel Bagley in Mesa. They weren't the first to make wine for sale—that would have probably been a farmer as a side business—but they were certainly the first to be doing enough of it on a regular basis that using the word winery would be accurate. They were already producing significant wine by 1884, and probably a year or two earlier, and by 1890 the Bagley vineyard had expanded to 30 acres." Other early winemakers included George Sirrine, one of Mesa's founding fathers, and Austrian immigrant Alois Cuber, who produced wines from his twenty-five-acre vineyard. By 1888, even California winemakers were starting to take notice, with James de Barth Shorb, founder of San Gabriel Wine Co., stating that Arizona wine was "equal age for age with California wine."

Unfortunately, the growth of Arizona's viticulture would face a more formidable challenge that could not be overcome. In November 1914, an amendment was passed banning the sale or manufacture of alcohol with a ballot that read:

> *Section 1. Ardent spirits, ale, beer, wine, or intoxicating liquor or liquors of whatever kind shall not be manufactured in, or introduced into the State of Arizona under any pretense. Every person who sells, exchanges, gives, barters, or disposes of any ardent spirits, ale, beer, wine, or intoxicating liquor of any kind, shall be guilty of a misdemeanor and upon conviction shall be imprisoned for not less than ten days nor more than two years, and fined not less than twenty-five dollars and costs nor more than three hundred dollars and costs for each offense; provided, that nothing in this amendment contained shall apply to the manufacture or sale of denatured alcohol.*

It also affected what could have been industry-propelling research being conducted by the University of Arizona in its early 1900s fruit trials, including the planting of wine grapes in Phoenix, Yuma and Tucson. "Several varieties of grapes were found suitable for wine manufacture," wrote W.H. Lawrence in a 1915 *Experiment Station* publication, but "recent legislation has apparently terminated the manufacture of wine within the state." As noted in Dr. Gordon Dutt's study "A Toast to Arizona Wines!," when the university vineyard was plowed under in 1933, over two hundred varieties of table and wine grapes were destroyed.

Already effectively silenced, with Prohibition and the ratification of the Eighteenth Amendment in 1920, Arizona's winegrowing industry would lay dormant for half a century before being reawakened by Dutt, a visionary soil scientist.

Chapter 3

Sonoita's Rebirth

SONOITA VINEYARDS

"I'm very original in my thinking, and at U of A, I was one of the few that did things differently and could get away with it," Dr. Gordon Dutt, founder of Sonoita Vineyards, says with a chuckle. Over a bottle of his namesake Buddy D's ZinGioVe, he's sharing the story of his accomplishments, which have led him to be acknowledged as the father of Arizona's modern-day wine industry.

Dutt came from the University of California–Davis to Arizona in 1964 after earning a bachelor of science degree at Montana State University and master of science and doctoral degrees in soil chemistry at Purdue. While working as a research irrigationist at the University of California–Davis, Dutt was hired by the University of Arizona to work on water quality. The topic of grape growing began with a discussion with horticulturist John Kuykendall. "When I came to the University of Arizona," he recalls, "I brought all of my contracts, including my main contract doing computer modeling with the Bureau of Reclamation. Our horticulturist, who was doing grape research, wanted me to go to Yuma for a lithium water quality problem. On our drive, I found out that there was not a single winery in Arizona. I was absolutely shocked." Having spent extensive time in California vineyards in his work at the University of California–Davis, Dutt was familiar with the terrain and climate found in wine country and saw similarities. "At that time,

Gordon Dutt at his home with a bottle of Buddy D's. *Author's collection.*

California was trying to get the world to believe, incorrectly, that the only thing important was climate. So, as I told our horticulturist, 'Hell, we've got any climate you want here. If you want a cooler climate, you go uphill. If you want a warmer climate, you go downhill.' And he agreed with me."

Looking for a way to incorporate grapes into his next project, Dutt applied for and received a grant to work on a water harvesting system for the growth of crops in arid climates. In 1972, he and his team planted wine grapes, a deep-rooted crop that required relatively little water, could survive moderate drought and contributed high economic value. The Page Ranch experimental plot between Tucson and Oracle Junction was chosen as the spot for the project due to its Whitehouse sandy loam soil, annual rainfall of eleven to sixteen inches and elevation of 3,680 feet. Twelve varieties were planted for a range that ripened early, mid- and late season: Barbera, Cabernet Sauvignon, Chardonnay, Chenin Blanc, Gamay, Pinot Noir, Ruby Cabernet, Sauvignon Blanc, White Riesling, Zinfandel, French Colombard and Sylvaner. Dutt implemented a salt treatment applied to the soil, allowing precipitation to collect in a reservoir below grapevine catchments. "I'm a chemist, so it was no problem for me to read up on how to make wine," says Dutt, "and being a soil scientist, I knew how to treat soil with sodium for runoff. We were growing grapes entirely on rainwater. The water would run off into a reservoir, and when needed, we would irrigate it back onto the plot. It was really something, it really was. We had all kinds of write-ups."

Sadly, as they prepared to make their first harvest two years later, Kuykendall passed away. "Oh, I felt terrible about that," says Dutt softly. "But we went ahead. I got a home winemaker's license because I couldn't make wine at the university, and we made wine from all these different varieties. And we were flabbergasted how well it turned out. We were absolutely flabbergasted. We really had picked the right place and the right soil to grow great grapes. Here we were getting these beautiful wines where supposedly we couldn't get anything but cactus juice," he laughs. "And so we had our first Arizona wine." In his seminal work "A Toast to Arizona Wines!" published by Dutt and his colleagues in 1976, he noted:

> *RESULTS: Surprising. The growth was good, the color was good and the taste was good—some as good as the best of the wines from the best regions of California....So we find that European wine grapes can produce excellent vintage in at least one area of Arizona, and premium quality wines achieved.*

"I put together a tasting panel," says Dutt, "and I included a reporter from the newspaper, which was a slick move, because she wrote up the whole thing. And from that write-up in the paper I got a call from the governor's office."

The four corner states of Arizona, New Mexico, Utah and Colorado had earlier formed a committee to explore new industries to stimulate economy across their adjacent regions, and now their interest was piqued to study the viability of vineyards. "The governor asked me if I would be interested in putting together a project on the production of wine, because the governors at that time wanted to get something new going. If you think I turned that down," he laughs, "you don't know me very well." In 1976, a $95,000 grant was approved for the Four Corners Grape Development Project.

"Also from that original newspaper article," he continues, "my great friend Blake Brophy came to see me and asked me if I would come down to Sonoita. He had spent all this time in Europe—I think he had been a correspondent for *Time* or *Life* magazine—and he thought Sonoita looked like wine country. He wanted to put in vineyards. I absolutely agreed with him, and so I put in a research vineyard in cooperation with the Babacomari Ranch in Sonoita."

Sonoita Vineyards, Arizona's oldest commercial vineyard and winery. *Sonoita Vineyards.*

By now, Dutt had been joined by horticulturist Dr. Eugene Mielke, and they were in search of a winemaker for the Four Corners project. Together they traveled to the University of California–Davis and spoke to the enology professor, who recommended one of his top graduate students, Wade Wolfe (now winemaker at Thurston Wolfe Winery in Washington State). "I think they were really planning on just farming him out and then hiring him back at Davis. But it didn't end up that way. We got the right person to work with, and he was pretty much in total agreement with everything that I had done up to that point."

The team, which included Dutt, Mielke, Wolfe and research assistant Sam Hughes, dove into the Four Corners project, working with universities in Colorado and New Mexico and the consulting firm overseeing the grape projects in Utah. Traveling to each state, they scouted both existing vineyards and new locations, choosing plots based on a variety of soil types, climate and altitudes to delineate the best areas for grape growing. In Arizona, Dutt had grapes planted in Page Ranch, Yuma, Safford, the Babacomari Ranch and Campbell Avenue Farm in Tucson, which housed the small university winery. "It was a fun project, great fun. We produced hundreds of wines from the Four Corners." In 1980, their findings were published in *Grape and Wine Production in the Four Corners Region*, confirming Arizona's potential to become a wine-growing area on par with other celebrated regions. "As far as I'm concerned, I did what I set out to do," says Dutt proudly, "and that was to show that we could indeed produce a world-class wine from Arizona grapes."

Dutt had compared the soil in Sonoita to Cote D'Or in Burgundy with its balance of acid, weathered clay and calcium carbonate and wasn't surprised when his studies showed that the Babacomari plot produced the best wine in the Four Corners study. In 1979, he leased the Babacomari Ranch land and started Viña Sonoita Vineyard. "As I told people at the time, I'm going to put my money where my mouth is," recalls Dutt. "And other people were interested. I had a group of South Africans and their friend Penny Edwards working with me, and we got the business going." He was speaking of South African native Adrian Hugo Bosman; his wife, Rosemary; Bosman's in-laws, Jon and Frances Harvey; and Penelope Edwards, who helped with the vineyard before starting Jon Hugo Vineyard. It was during this time that Dutt received a letter from Leon Adams, the acclaimed writer and founder of the Wine Institute. "He told me that if you're going to have a grape business in Arizona, you have to pass a farm winery law. I took this to Blake and his brother Frank Brophy, who was a lawyer, and they got things going and put it to the legislation. As Blake told me, 'The wholesalers will fight you tooth and nail, but you'll get support from agriculture and you'll win out with them behind you.' He was exactly right. And we think this helped too—the funny part is Frank Brophy was the bridge partner of the president of the Senate," he says with an amused smile, "and he worked with us because he was Frank's buddy. The Arizona Farm Winery Law passed, and I went ahead and put in the winery with the vineyard."

In 1983, Dutt founded Sonoita Vineyards Winery, initially with a cooperative arrangement between Edwards, the Bosmans and the Harveys. Although Robert Webb had already launched Arizona's first licensed winery since Prohibition in Tucson and Bill Staltari had opened the second in northern Arizona outside Camp Verde, Dutt's was the first winery to source from an Arizona vineyard. "The Brophys helped me a lot," says Dutt. "They were very influential." And in fact, Blake Brophy was responsible for drafting the application for Sonoita to be recognized as Arizona's first official American Viticultural Area designation in 1984.

In his 1976 study results, Dutt closes with the hopeful wish that "one day an American president may propose to his honored guests a toast in chianti—Arizona chianti." Little did he know the part he would play in his foreshadowing, although it would be with an Arizona Cabernet Sauvignon and Fumé Blanc. In 1989, his wines were selected by *Los Angeles Times* wine critic Robert Balzar to be served at the inauguration festivities for George H.W. Bush. "They invited the best winemakers from all the states to bring wine to the inauguration. My wife was still alive at the time and she was in a wheelchair, but she could still dance with me. We danced right up to the stage and got close to the new president," Dutt reminisces. "That was one of the biggest thrills of my life."

The Modern-Day Wine Industry Is Launched

In the Sonoita-Elgin area, Sonoita Vineyards would become the epicenter. "Gordon Dutt had the facility, and most of us subleased space from him," recalls Gary Ellam, owner of Village of Elgin Winery, one of the early establishments. "I remember Reid Martin back in the day at Sonoita Vineyards producing the first sparkling wines to come out of Arizona, including the first blanc de noir and blanc de blanc. Essentially, that first Sonoita wine group all started making wine at Sonoita Vineyards, whether it was at Jon Hugo barn or the new building that Sonoita Vineyards is in now."

Ellam's winery in Elgin, the small town adjacent to Sonoita, was founded by Bill LeTarte along with his daughter Kathy, Ellam's wife. "Back then," says Ellam, "the winery was Bill, Kathy and myself. Which made Kathy the first female winemaker in the state. She's been doing it for thirty-five years." The couple has since grown the Village of Elgin to include Tombstone and Four Monkey wines and added a brewery and distillery which routinely produce award-winning wines and spirits. LeTarte, who also founded Arizona's first wine festival, acted as managing partner and "marketing genius," says Ellam, until 1995, when the Ellams bought him out and became sole owners. When LeTarte passed away in 2016, he left behind a legacy of co-founding the region's first wine festival, the Sonoita-Elgin Merchants Chamber of Commerce and the *Vintage Voice* trade publication.

"The industry has done this wave pattern," Ellam observed. "In the beginning, you had the smaller guys that were all sharing equipment and

Kathy and Gary Ellam of Village of Elgin Winery. *Author's collection.*

sharing a common interest and goals. It kind of slumped off a little, and then it started to build up again." The passing of the Domestic Farm Winery Bill in 1982 ushered in the launching of new wineries and vineyards in the region: Warren Brown's Rincon Valley Vineyards, Dick Eastman's Fort Bowie Vineyards, Sue and Tom Brady's Terra Rossa Vineyard, Thomas Peabody's Whetstone Vineyard, Harold and Karen Callaghan's Callaghan Vineyards and more. Ellam ticks off some of the earliest pioneers: "You had Tino Ocheltree and Arizona Vineyards, Don Minchella with Kokopelli and Mark Stern with Paradise Valley Winery. There was Santa Cruz Winery, which I think was the first kosher winery west of the Mississippi; Zvi Naveh, Oliver and Lynnette Weisel were the owners at that time, with Rabbi Yossie Shem Tov in Tucson making all the kosher wine."

"Of course, when Prohibition killed everything, it was tough going to get the industry back up and running once the repeal came in," continues Ellam. "But you've got those pioneering navy guys. The guys that did the foundation and groundwork were all navy guys. Gordon was in the navy in World War II, Bob Webb was a P3 pilot, I was in the navy, Bill LeTarte was in the navy, Tino was in the navy. It's that spirit. Us damn dirty sailors will try anything, especially if it includes alcohol," he laughs. "All of them should be recognized. People like Bill LeTarte, Tino Ocheltree and Bill Staltari were all integral founding parts of this industry. I believe you have to honor the history and traditions.

"Some of them have come and gone, but now we're at this huge upswing, which is great for the industry. If somebody had told you a hundred years ago that some of the best whiskey in the country was coming out of Arizona, you'd call him a liar and punch him in the teeth," laughs Ellam, whose Arizona Straight Bourbon Whiskey has won multiple gold medals at the San Francisco World Spirits Competition and New York International Spirits Competition. "And it's the same thing with the wine. If somebody had told you forty years ago that Arizona wineries would win back-to-back Jefferson Cups or that Sam Pillsbury would be getting four double golds at the San Francisco competition, you wouldn't believe it. I mean, the products are there. They shine, they do everything they're supposed to do. It'd be nice if we got a little bit more media recognition. It'd be nice if the state promoted the products a little bit better. But you also have to do the work yourself."

Meanwhile, another vineyard was planting its roots in Sonoita, one that would propel Arizona on to the national stage when it received a score of ninety-four from esteemed wine critic Robert Parker of the *Wine Advocate*, making it the highest-rated Arizona wine of the time.

CALLAGHAN VINEYARDS

"It was my dad's idea," says Kent Callaghan, owner of Callaghan Vineyards, as he pours a glass of his Tannat, a Basque red wine grape. He is sharing the story of how he ended up in Elgin as one of the region's most accomplished and respected winemakers. His parents, Harold and Karen, lived in Sonoita but owned a summer house in British Columbia on Galliano Island. One year, they learned that an island neighbor named Jim McDonald was teaching classes in home winemaking. Knowing that wine was being made in the Sonoita-Elgin area, Kent's father enrolled. "They bought a house here in the same year that Gordon was planting his vineyards, and there was a huge amount of publicity and media attention, so they knew about that," says Callaghan. "My dad would pick wild blackberries on the island and make fruit wines, and he enjoyed the process quite a bit." That fall, the Callaghans took a detour to Napa and the Sonoma Valley before coming home to Sonoita. They returned to Napa with their son the following February, and their decision was made. "My dad got the bug, and they never

Lisa and Kent Callaghan of Callaghan Vineyards. *Becky Limberg.*

looked anywhere else," says Kent Callaghan. "They ended up buying the land in 1988 after taking me to Napa to sell me on the idea."

Callaghan had recently graduated from college with a degree in philosophy and completed some graduate school, but it didn't take much to convince him to join his family on their new venture. "I like working outside, and I loved it down here. I would come down here all the time on weekends. It's a great place to live, beautiful, quiet." For Callaghan, who at this point was not even much of a wine drinker, education was the next step, and the new business partners enrolled in extension courses at the University of California–Davis, along with partaking in wine-imbibing research. "We also put in a restaurant the same spring we put the vineyard in and did a lot of eating and drinking," laughs Callaghan.

They planted their current vineyard in 1990, starting with seventeen acres and choosing Bordeaux varietals, which was the accepted premise for new wine regions. "That was just what you did," says Callaghan. "We did plant Merlot and Cabernet Franc as well, and then two acres of Zinfandel, which turned out to be a nightmare. But we also had three acres in what was originally an experimental plot that had all kinds of stuff—Grenache,

Mourvedre, Barbera, Nebbiolo, Pinot Gris, Marzan and Clairette, a weird white that buds late and is tough. We've got quite a bit of it out there now."

Observing the grapes that grew well, they realized that they didn't want to focus on the usual varieties. As Callaghan explains it, they had nine acres of Cabernet but learned that the heavy clay coupled with summer rains wasn't the best soil type for that variety. "It was better for Merlot, actually, and Merlot in the early days was our best fruit because it was more suited to the place. It just became obvious over time that there were other things that we should be looking at, so our first solid new variety was Mourvedre, which was the first planting of that in the state." In 1997, Callaghan tore out the original vines in the experimental section, replanted with Mourvedre and renamed it Claire's plot after his youngest daughter.

"It's hilarious. People asked me, 'What the hell did you plant that for?'" he recounts. "Nobody can pronounce it. Nobody knows what it is. But that's one advantage of selling wine direct out of your tasting room. Because you can explain what it is. If you've never tasted it, but you like it a lot, then it's actually a selling point that it's a weird variety nobody's ever heard of."

And tasting room visitors weren't the only fans of Callaghan wines. In the August 1994 issue of the *Wine Advocate*, Robert Parker scored not one, but three Callaghan Vineyard wines ninety points: The 1992 Buena Suerte Sonoita Cabernet Sauvignon, the 1992 Whetstone/Redtail Sonoita Chardonnay and the 1992 Redtail Sonoita blend. In December's issue, Parker declared him one of the best winemakers in the world, and the following year he compared Callaghan's 1993 Chardonnay to a Domaine de la Romanee–Conti Montrachet, rating it as Arizona's first ninety-four-point wine. Since Parker put a spotlight on Callaghan, the accolades have grown, and medals continue to stack up.

Currently, Callaghan and his wife, Lisa, cultivate a twenty-five-acre vineyard with grapes that skew more toward Mediterranean and Spanish, including Graciano, Mourvedre and Grenache. More experimentation for what is best suited to Sonoita's unique terrain and climate has led to Tannat, first planted in 2008. "It buds out relatively early, but even when they get frosted a little, they tend to come back out," notes Callaghan, "and the quality of the wine is really good and distinctive."

But these successful years in the Sonoita AVA have not been without their hardships. Callaghan talks about a "gloomy period" in the mid-1990s to 2002 with neglected vineyards, in part due to the difficulties with calcium carbonate in the calcareous soil. Dutt remembers a devastating period in the early 1990s when his vineyards were struck by back-to-back infestations

Award-winning wines at the Callaghan Vineyards tasting room. *Author's collection.*

of Texas root rot, a fungus that attacks the roots and causes plant wilt, and Pierce's disease, a deadly bacteria spread by insects that once wiped out forty thousand acres of wine grapes in California. "We were doing absolutely great through '89 and '90, and then we had this terrible hit with Texas root rot," he recalls. "That, we knew how to handle, but then we got Pierce's disease. We didn't realize it was in there; it wiped our vineyard out, and we had to start all over again. It was terrible for us, but thank God Kent Callaghan kept it going and kept making quality wines. I'm real grateful to Kent." In 2010, a May freeze saw the temperature drop to twenty-eight degrees and hover for four hours in Sonoita, splitting grapevines and wiping out tender vines beginning to bud. Any plants that did recover were ravaged by a decimating hailstorm with sixty-mile-per-hour winds that August.

SONOITA'S WINE REGION GROWS

But Arizona winegrowers are a passionate, tenacious bunch; "a short memory also helps," says Callaghan. Lessons are learned, new techniques are employed and another season arrives.

Visit Sonoita wine country today and you'll find a multitude of tasting rooms scattered among vineyards. There's Kief Manning's Kief-Joshua Vineyards; Anne Roncone's Lightning Ridge Cellars; Karyl Wilhelm's Wilhelm Family Vineyards; Milton and Susan Craig's Charron Vineyards & Winery; Phil and Kim Asmundson's Deep Sky Vineyard; Mark Beres, Marc Moeller and Tom Kitchens's Flying Leap Vineyards and Distillery; James Callahan's Rune Wines; Jim and Ann Gardner's Hannah's Hill Vineyard; the Bostocks' Dos Cabezas WineWorks; Chris and Breanna Hamilton's Rancho Rossa Vineyards; Pavle and Carla Milic's Los Milics Winery and Vineyards; Stephen Basila's Autumn Sage Vineyard; the Ellams' Village of Elgin Winery; and Shannon Zouzoulas and Megan Haller's Arizona Hops and Vines.

At Rune Wines, set in the rolling hills of Sonoita's grasslands, James Callahan is pouring award-winning wines fermented with wild yeast and graced with labels in his distinctive wood-cut designs. Honing his skills in Washington State and New Zealand, he was cellar master at California's Kosta Browne when *Wine Spectator* magazine named its Pinot Noir wine of the year. "He's super smart, he's very resourceful, he knows what he's doing and he's inventive," says fellow winemaker Sam Pillsbury of Pillsbury Wine Company. After a year as winemaker at Aridus, Callahan purchased

Arizona Hops and Vines in Sonoita. *Kylie Daniels.*

Flying Leap Vineyards and Distillery with dormant grapes. *Author's collection.*

a twenty-seven-acre property in 2013, and his Quonset hut tasting room offers visitors a striking view of the Willcox playa.

Just next door to Callaghan is the Flying Leap tasting room and adjacent distillery. Flying Leap Vineyards was formed by three best friends and former U.S. Air Force pilots: Mark Beres, Marc Moeller and Tom Kitchens. Founded in 2010, it was originally planned as a small-scale winery. "Mark Beres was just going to get a few acres over in Willcox," relates Kitchens, "and it was going to be his hobby to make wine for himself and to give away at Christmas to family and friends. Then Marc came along and said, hey, let's make a business out of this, and the few acres went to twenty acres. Then I came along, and the twenty-acre plan grew to sixty acres in Willcox." In 2012, the partners bought Canelo Hills vineyard from Tim and Joan Mueller with a three-thousand-square-foot facility and a ten-acre plot located next to Callaghan Vineyards, where they also built a new distillery.

Dos Cabezas WineWorks

Little did Todd Bostock know when he took his first sip of Dos Cabezas wine in 2002 that a mere four years later, he and his wife, Kelly, would become the proud owners of Dos Cabezas WineWorks, soon garner winemaking awards and be recognized nationally, including among the *San Francisco Chronicle's* 10 Winemakers to Watch.

An Arizona native, Todd Bostock's background spanned studies in science and art and working in a print store before pursuing a wine career with University of California–Davis extension classes. Like many enthusiasts looking to get into the field, he had his eye on California. That all changed in the fall of 2002, when Bostock poured himself a glass of Dos Cabezas wine and realized that there was something special happening in his home state. "That's what planted the seed that I could do this in Arizona," Bostock recounts as he stacks bottles of a new vintage of sparkling wine. At the time, his courses at UC Davis included a section on regional American wines. "I decided to buy some Arizona wine to try, so I bought a bottle of Dos Cabezas at AJ's. I remember I was in the backyard of my house in central Phoenix, the sun was going down and it tasted as good as anything I'd had, but totally different. It was so exciting to me."

"I started tracking it down right away," Bostock says. "I saw Dos Cabezas was doing a tasting locally, and I talked to Sam Pillsbury, found out they were doing another tasting in Sonoita the following weekend and drove down to meet Frank [DiChristofano] and Al [Buhl]. I offered to work for Frank, and he called me the next Monday."

While maintaining his full-time job, Bostock volunteered his services as an apprentice at Dos Cabezas, working as an assistant winemaker with head winemaker DiChristofano to gain experience and knowledge of the process. "That started right after the harvest in October of 2002, lasted through the summer, and I became the winemaker before the harvest of 2003." At the age of twenty-five, he stepped into his new role when DiChristofano retired, with Bostock's pay consisting of salary and equity in the company. Bostock was also working toward his goal of becoming an independent winemaker and in 2003 bought Pronghorn Vineyard in Sonoita. Industrious and ambitious, at this time he was juggling his time and commuting between his print and graphics job, Dos Cabezas and Pronghorn Vineyard. "I was working at all three," Bostock recalls. "I ended up moving to Tucson at one point, which was kind of in the middle, so I'd spend a couple of days in Phoenix, a couple of days in Willcox and a couple of days in Sonoita, and I did that until 2006."

In 2006, with the aid of his parents, Bostock and his wife, Kelly, purchased Dos Cabezas WineWorks and moved the winery to Sonoita. In addition to Pronghorn, they also now own Cimarron Vineyard in the Kansas Settlement, which they purchased from pioneering Oregon winemaker Dick Erath (the

Todd and Kelly Bostock of Dos Cabezas WineWorks. *Becky Limberg.*

original Dos Cabezas Vineyard is owned by Maynard Keenan and has been renamed the Al Buhl Memorial Vineyard). "We have fifteen acres planted in Sonoita and thirty-seven acres in Willcox," says Bostock. Varieties include Syrah, Piquepoul Blanc, Aglianico and Petit Verdot. Dos Cabezas is one of the most widely recognized Arizona labels, and its releases include the 2015 Águileón, which received Best in Show at the 2018 azcentral Arizona Wine Competition and received ninety-three points from wine critic James Suckling. A refined blend of Tempranillo, Graciano, Cabernet Sauvignon, Cabernet Franc and Petite Sirah, it's cleverly named for their youngest son Griffin—a combination of the Spanish words for eagle (*águila*) and lion (*león*), the two animals that create the mythical creature called a griffin.

The Bostocks strive to create distinctive wines representative of Arizona, "wines that go with the food and the climate," says Bostock. "What are people going to want in Phoenix in the summertime when it's 110? That's what I think our job is, and then we find the grapes that can consistently produce wines that fit that bill. People should know that Arizona wine belongs on the table, it has a place there, it's unique and distinctive and I think that's exciting."

A LEGACY CONTINUES

At Sonoita Vineyards, Gordon Dutt's granddaughter Lori Reynolds maintains the family legacy as the current winemaker. "My first memories are literally being carried on my grandpa's shoulders throughout the vineyard," Reynolds recalls. "I remember labeling wine with paper labels when I was seven and playing in the winery on top of the pallets pretending they were my ships and my castles." She took a circuitous route, however, to end up as the winemaker. Attending the University of Arizona, Reynolds graduated with a bachelor's degree in veterinary science with a minor in chemistry but had already decided on a change in career. As she contemplated her next field of study, Dutt spoke up at a family gathering. "My grandpa, one Christmas, just said, 'You were born to make wine. Why don't you?' He had heard that UC Davis had an online wine school, someone said Karyl Wilhelm had taken the classes, and so we went over to Karyl's winery. Even though she had a tour that day, she was kind enough to take the time to talk to my grandfather, me and my dad." Reynolds enrolled in 2012 and started from the ground up. "I became a jack-of-all-trades. I'd clean the gutters, scrub the floors, I did everything." As assistant winemaker, she also mentored under the tutelage of winemaker Fran Lightly. "I learned from him, and his wife had an amazing palate, so I learned quite a bit from her too."

In 2013, Lightly retired, and it was time for Reynolds to take the reins. At twenty-six years old, this made her the youngest female winemaker in the state. "I hadn't finished all of my courses, so I was excited and nervous," she says, but she received the community's support. She recalls that Megan Haller, their former assistant winemaker who had left to start Hops & Vines, "raced over here a couple of days after he had left and said, 'Whatever you need, I will come and help you.'" Kent Callaghan also lent his expertise, mentoring her for a year and sharing his wisdom and experience. "We would taste barrels, and he would say 'Okay, this is how California does it and this is how you're taught at UC Davis. But this is how it needs to be done in Arizona, so we don't care what they do. This is how it works for us. You were taught this, let's take that and mold it.' He was amazing."

Joined by her husband, Robi Reynolds, who took over as vineyard manager, Lori makes wine from mostly French varietals. For her grandfather, she grows Sangiovese, his favorite grape, and bottles a special blend of Sangiovese and Zinfandel called Buddy D's ZinGioVe. "It's a really nice light-bodied red, a great little table wine."

Winemaker Lori Reynolds looks on as her grandfather Dr. Gordon Dutt is honored at the Arizona Wine Founders' Dinner. *Courtesy of Mike Pigford.*

Two of the most interesting wines being made at Sonoita Vineyards are a taste of history via the famous Mission grape. One is a red wine called, fittingly, Mission. "It's very astringent, so I leave about 1½ to 2 percent residual sugar in it," Reynolds explains. "Not sweet enough to make it overly sweet, but enough to mellow out the astringency. Every vintage is a little bit different, and the '16 is what we have right now. It finishes dry and has a lot of pepper, clove and some red fruit. It's just really interesting and different."

She also makes a special communion wine called Angel Wings, commissioned by one of Gordon Dutt's close friends, Father Greg Adolf, who for the last forty years has blessed the vineyard at an annual celebration. Father Adolf approached Dutt about serving a historic communion grape, the cuttings were planted in 1997 and Dutt made his first mission wine in 2000. "I think it was about five hundred gallons just for the church," says Reynolds. "But Father Greg said, 'It's too red and stains our white linens, and we need something sweeter, it's too dry.'" At that time, Sonoita Vineyards was sourcing French Colombard from the Fort Bowie Vineyard, so Dutt bottled a blend of Mission with the Colombard to make a pink wine fermented with some residual sugar. "Well," says Reynolds, "the congregation kept coming over here asking to buy communion wine, the

Sonoita Vineyards Angel Wings ready for labeling. *Author's collection.*

church ladies liked it because it didn't stain the white linens and everyone was happy. I change the whites depending on the quantity of grapes and this year made it with Malvasia Bianca. Now we make about one thousand gallons a year, and it sells out every time."

A NEW VINEYARD TAKES ROOT

As Arizona wines continue to collect more national awards and international acclaim, the future looks bright for Arizona's first AVA. It's rare to have the opportunity to see a vineyard and winery being born, but that is exactly what is happening at Los Milics Winery and Vineyards.

Pavle Milic is the engaging beverage director and co-owner of lauded FnB restaurant in Old Town Scottsdale. In addition to chef and partner Charleen Badman's 2019 James Beard award win as Best Chef: Southwest, he has earned a Beard award nomination himself for his wine program, which also introduced the first curated all-Arizona wine list. As an early supporter of Arizona's viticultural treasures, his efforts have come full circle as he and his wife, Carla, have broken ground on Sonoita's newest winery, slated to open in late 2019. His current Los Milics wines are a collaboration with Dos Cabezas WineWorks, but this will be a new label, with his own vineyards and Carla as winemaker.

"One of the reasons we chose this place is because of those mountains," says Carla Milic as she gestures across the newly tilled field in the direction of a view backdropped by the Mustang Mountain range. The twenty-acre ranch will be planted with thirteen acres of vines, with construction to start on a production facility, tasting room, restaurant and guest casitas. The striking architecture will incorporate Sonoran desert views and be designed by Chen + Suchart Studio, chosen by Pavle Milic, who met the couple as regulars at the restaurant. "Pavle always said if we had something to build one day, they were going to be the architects," remembers Carla. Casitas will boast glass roofs to admire starry skies, and overnight guests will be able to dine at the winery restaurant. "It's going to be really nice to have the people who make the wine also cook for you and create experiences," says Milic.

"But you know what? The tasting room can be awesome, but if we don't make you feel good, then all this amazingness doesn't matter," Milic says

Carla Milic at the future site of Los Milics Winery and Vineyards. *Author's collection.*

as she points at blueprints and renderings on the dining room table of their cozy ranch house. "For example, if you visit Callaghan's tasting room, it's simple, but when you're there, you feel like the most important person in the world. That's the way Lisa makes you feel, and that's what we want to do. Some people will want to go to the tasting room, taste wines and leave, and some will want a more intimate experience, spend time in their casita and eat at the restaurant. We want everyone to feel comfortable." The Milics are already the owners of a fourteen-acre vineyard in Elfrida called Jenny's (named after Pavle's grandmother) planted with Tempranillo, Graciano, Garnacha and Mourvedre, with a plan to open the new winery in the fall of 2019.

When approached by investors who were regulars at FnB to partner in this project, the Milics knew their lives were about to change. "We had talked about making wine one day," Carla Milic says, "but it was always far in the future." But the future became now, and the Milics had to make a decision. "Even though we are a team and do everything together," Milic says, "Pavle is more the one to handle the marketing, tasting room and restaurant, and he said, 'I need you to be the winemaker.'"

Milic agreed and started working in Jenny's Vineyard, knowing that she was embarking on a tough but rewarding journey. "One of the big sacrifices was the seven months I traveled from Chandler down here, every day, Tuesday to Friday," says Milic. "I had to drive three hours each way—wake up at three or four, work, come home, eat dinner with my son, then go to sleep at seven and start all over again. It was tiring but made me stronger." Moving to the ranch house at the site of the vineyard eased the long commute but not her work ethic. Milic plans on taking courses at UC Davis, but in this supportive arena, she is receiving an invaluable viticulture education being mentored by some of the most knowledgeable people in the industry: Nikki Check, the former director of viticulture at Yavapai College; Kent Callaghan; and the Bostocks. "With Nikki, every time we do something, it's a class, and Todd is my university now. I'm very thankful for Kent, Lisa, Todd, Kelly. They're always telling us, if you have any doubts, if you have any questions, please ask. So we've been lucky to have people that support us and know that we're new. They know what they've gone through before and try to help us not make the same mistakes, even though we know there are going to be mistakes."

"And we are so blessed to be around friends," Milic continues. "When I moved here, the first day we worked on the house, Pavle had to leave and I was alone with my son. Lisa sent me a message, 'Do you need anything?'

Los Milics wine will make way for the new Los Milics Winery and Vineyards wine labels. *Author's collection.*

Are you okay?' Then Kelly, 'What do you need? Can I help you?' That is the energy here, and that is what we want to try to do too."

"We really want to be a part of the community and not just Los Milics. We want to have dinners here and bring in guest winemakers like Todd and Kent and James [Callahan]. We have so many ideas. It's a lot of work, but it's satisfying. And it's beautiful," says Milic earnestly. "It's beautiful because you are building something for the future. Our kids are going to look back and say, oh wow, my parents did this. We're very excited to have everyone come and see what Los Milics has to offer."

Chapter 4

Wine Industry Rebirth: Willcox

Willcox is considered an enclosed basin, meaning no water flows through it and it is fed by rain and an underground aquifer. Sitting at a slightly lower elevation than Sonoita, it now boasts the largest acreage of vineyards, supplying over 75 percent of the grapes grown in Arizona. It was recognized as Arizona's newest American Viticultural Area in 2016. Winegrowers are drawn to the unique climate, which has been compared to Argentina; fairly inexpensive land costs; and soils of sandy loam and alluvial deposits. It is home to the Willcox Playa, an ancient lake bed, and the fertile Willcox Bench. In "Geology of the Willcox AVA" on his AZ Wine Monk website, Cody Burkett describes the terroir:

> *At its greatest extent, the lake was likely about 35 feet deep, and 75 square miles. The lake left behind fertile shores and beach ridges at this extent, where soils and rock that had eroded from the mountain were mixed together by wave action from wind and water. It is one of these ancient beach ridges that forms the present Willcox Bench....Red wines made from grapes grown on the Bench always smell to me like the dust from the dirt roads that criss-cross this area; whites seem to pick up the minerality and limestone from the caliche layers left behind by the lake, and possess intense floral notes as well.*

ROBERT WEBB

Former navy pilot Robert Webb opened the Tucson Hobby Shop in the early 1970s and in May 1980 graduated his hobby winemaking events to the R.W. Webb Winery, claiming the title of the first bonded winery in Arizona since Prohibition. Without a vineyard at that time, he sourced grapes from California and New Mexico. In his 2010 *AZ Wine Lifestyle* article titled "Grape Perspectives: 30 Years Too Soon," he shares his firsthand account of his winemaking journey. "People told me that I was out of my mind. 'What was I going to do, make wine out of cactus? This is Arizona, not California.' 'You're just an ex-Navy pilot and a home winemaker with no formal training, who do you think you are?'" But, as fellow navy man and winemaker Gary Ellam has said, these navy men are a fearless bunch.

According to Webb, because of Bureau of Alcohol, Tobacco, Firearms and Explosives (ATF) regulations, even though the wine was produced in Tucson, an Arizona designation could not be put on the label. Webb was restricted to "American," and thus his first label read "American Cabernet Sauvignon," made with grapes grown in Paso Robles, California. As he recounts further in his article:

> *State law at that time said that an Arizona winery could only sell wine to a distributor. You could not sell to anyone else—not to a restaurant, not to a store, not to a tasting room, only to licensed wine distributors. I hadn't thought things through very well. What if no distributor wanted to buy my wine? 1200 cases is a lot of wine to drink, even with the help of friends. Luckily, All American Distributors purchased all 1200 cases for $50,000. I thought I had died and gone to heaven—I was overjoyed. In 1981 we produced 1500 cases of Cabernet from California.*

Inspired by Dutt's success with the Four Corners study, in 1981, Webb began looking for land to grow his own grapes. Although he didn't have the funds, he was able to partner with investors and knew what he was looking for. "It had to have a good water supply, high elevation for cool nights, no Texas root rot and be affordable. I found what I thought was the perfect site in the Sulphur Springs Valley on the slope of the Dos Cabezas Mountains near Willcox, Arizona. It met all of my criteria." Webb continues:

> *By 1982 there were a handful of crazy people who had planted grapes. Bill Staltari founded the second winery—San Dominique and Gordon*

Young grapevines. *Becky Limberg.*

> *Dutt founded the third—Sonoita Vineyards. It became apparent to us that we needed to get the law changed so that we could sell our wine direct, bypassing the 3-tier system or we would forever be at the mercy of the powerful distributors. That is when we founded the Arizona Wine Growers Association. Dr. Adrian Bozeman was our first president. I was on the original board as was Bill Staltari and Warren Brown.*

Like others, with the passage of the Domestic Farm Winery Bill, Webb was ready to move forward. In 1984, he purchased a forty-acre plot and planted his first vineyard with twenty acres of grapes, including Cabernet Sauvignon, Merlot and Petite Sirah. Soon, he had doubled his production and continued to expand, opening a new winery and tasting room in 1986.

"I learned that to be successful as an Arizona winery you had to do more than make good wine," he wrote. "You had to make good wine out of Arizona fruit and market, market, market the wine. By the time I sold the winery in 1997, I had RW Webb wines in every supermarket chain in the state." In 1989, Webb sold his original vineyard to Al Buhl, another pioneer who was instrumental in developing the Willcox wine region. Though Buhl, a civilian personnel manager for the U.S. Army base at Fort Huachuca at the time, had little experience with winegrowing, he was inspired by Dutt's remarkable findings and left his own legacy when he passed away in 2014.

AL BUHL AND DOS CABEZAS

"He was a visionary," says his wife, Ann Buhl. "He put his whole heart in it and just loved being in the vineyard. He thought, you know, it's God's grace. You're nurturing these plants in the earth, you get the fruit off the vine at harvest time and then you make these glorious wines."

Buhl's interest in viticulture was born in the Finger Lakes wine region of New York. A Staten Island native, he attended college at Syracuse in upstate New York. "But he didn't have the money to go back to the city on spring break," says Ann. "One of his classmates' family owned vineyards in the Finger Lakes region, and Al started going home with him and working in their family's vineyard. That's what stayed with him."

She remembers stopping at Arizona Vineyards and their surprise to discover wine was being made in Arizona. Buhl started researching. At the time, the Buhls were working at Fort Huachuca and living in Sierra Vista. Ann clearly remembers a pivotal leisurely drive. "You could go out the West Gate through Fort Huachuca the back way over the mountain and you're in Sonoita. And we went out the gate and I'm like, God, this is beautiful out here! Where are we? He was telling me about his research, and then all of a sudden we came upon a winery, and I said, are you kidding me? Sonoita Vineyards was just this little tiny place, like a house. We tasted wines, Dr. Dutt showed us around and Al talked to him for what seemed like an eternity," she remembers with a chuckle. In 1989, the Buhls purchased Robert Webb's forty-acre vineyard.

As Al Buhl wrote in his article "Perspectives on the Arizona Wine Industry 1990–2013" for *AZ Wine Lifestyle*, "Back when Gordon Dutt (and company) generated interest in the area through their Four Corners Study, it seemed that anyone with the slightest interest in wine grape growing or winemaking could jump right in and take advantage of our wonderful climate, as well as our abundant and affordable land, and become a 'gentleman farmer.'" He soon found out he was in for an "unbelievably steep learning curve." Arming himself with research references such as Jancis Robinson's book *Vines, Grapes & Wines* and *Practical Winery & Vineyard Journals*, he spoke to everyone he could who was able to share his or her experience and knowledge.

Buhl describes his vineyard decisions:

> *Because only 20 of the 40 acres had been planted, I had to decide the appropriate varieties for the remaining acreage. I wanted to grow grapes that would produce the wines that I personally liked, but I also wanted to*

develop grapes that would grow well in this specific terroir of the vineyard site. My mantra became somewhat existential at that point (maybe from hanging around too much with philosophy major Kent Callaghan), it was essentially, "This above all, to thine own site be true!" This was not an easy task and I was quickly finding out how little I knew.

In his article, he mentioned sage advice he received from winemaker Paola D'Andrea to "understand that each site had its own peculiar needs and specific growing requirements, and that any expert advice had to be taken with a grain of salt. In other words, what worked well in California, Oregon, Italy or Australia, would not necessarily work here in Arizona." Buhl took this information to heart. "He was a visionary as far as what varietals to plant," his wife shares. "Everybody was planting the same kind of grapes—the Cabernets, the Sauvignon Blancs—but he was into the Italian and Spanish varietals like Tempranillo, Sangiovese and Malvasia Bianca. Not all of them made it, but the ones that did, they thrived."

Successful harvests soon followed, and Buhl would sell grapes to area wineries such as Santa Cruz, Terra Rossa, Paradise Valley, Village of Elgin, Sonoita Vineyards and Callaghan Vineyards. For those early years, Buhl concentrated on his beloved vineyard until he "had" to open a winery. By this time, the Buhls were living in Elgin, and Ann shares an amusing anecdote:

Arizona wine grapes. *Becky Limberg.*

"Around 1992, we had such a huge crop of Cabernet that we hadn't sold it all. Santa Cruz and Kent Callaghan loaned us winemaking equipment, and we made what I affectionately call garage wine. I have pictures of my son Matthew—he was only about six—punching down the grapes. Just for grins, we entered it in the 1994 State Fair, and I still have the blue ribbon and the check for three dollars we won," she says with a laugh.

In 1995, Buhl formed Dos Cabezas WineWorks with Kent Callaghan, Bob Loew, Jon Marcus and Don and Katherine Magowan, first with Kent Callaghan as winemaker ("Kent did a dry Riesling that I would kill for," recalls Ann Buhl) and later Frank DiChristofano. Assistant winemaker Todd Bostock would later join the team before purchasing his own vineyards and the Dos Cabezas WineWorks label.

But until then, Al Buhl observed:

> *Gradually…very gradually…the Arizona wine industry began getting recognized, not simply as a novelty, but seriously recognized. Sonoita Vineyards' 1989 Cabernet Sauvignon was well received. Callaghan Vineyards caught the attention of Robert Parker for their 1992 Fume Blanc and their 1991 Cabernet Sauvignon. Dos Cabezas won awards in the "New World Wine Competition" for its Riesling and Chardonnay. Other awards and recognition followed, which included both Callaghan Vineyards and Dos Cabezas being selected for events at the White House during different administrations.*

Willcox today is home to over fifteen vineyards, wineries and tasting rooms. Among them, you'll find Tom and Edie Gustason's High Lonesome Vineyard; Jim and Ruth Graham's Golden Rule Vineyards; Greg Gonnerman's Laramita Cellars; John McLoughlin's Cellar 433; Todd Myers and Michelle Minta's Rhumb Line Vineyard; Jason Domanico's Passion Cellars and Salvatore Vineyards; Mark and Jacque Cook's Coronado Vineyards; Mark Beres, Marc Moeller and Tom Kitchens's Flying Leap Vineyards; the Carlsons' Carlson Creek Vineyard; Rod Keeling and Jan Schaefer's Keeling Schaefer Vineyards; Scott and Joan Dahmer's Aridus Wine Company; Rob and Sarah Hammelman's Sand-Reckoner Vineyards; Sam Pillsbury's Pillsbury Wine Company; the Pierce family's Bodega Pierce and Saeculum Cellars; Chad and Monica Preston's Birds and Barrels Vineyards; and Rhona MacMillan and Mark Jorve's Zarpara Vineyard. Harold and Katie Christ's Windmill Winery, an hour north of Tucson, also has Willcox ties, producing Windmill Winery Wines through John McLoughlin's Odyssey Cellars.

PILLSBURY WINE COMPANY

The foundation of Webb's and Buhl's viticulture work gave rise to more vignerons arriving to play their part in building Arizona's wine region. For those spreading the word about the Grand Canyon State's blossoming industry, Sam Pillsbury's reaction to a glass of Arizona wine was ideal. He fell in love and promptly bought a vineyard.

Pillsbury, a famous Hollywood and New Zealand film director and now winemaker, leans back in his chair as he talks about his award-winning wine and stacks of medals. His home office is as multifaceted as his personality. Behind him, art hangs on the wall. There's a piece by acclaimed Maori artist Ralph Hotere ("I made a documentary about him in 1974") next to a proudly displayed childhood painting by his young son.

"Ever since I was a kid, I've loved wine," says Pillsbury. He vividly remembers traveling on an Italian ocean liner with his parents as a thirteen-year-old where wine was freely poured. "Those Chiantis on the table every night, spicy and fragrant, glowing ruby red when held up to the light, parents drinking at my side, wine with dinner, a little buzz on…I was in heaven," he wrote in a *Phoenix New Times* column. His love of wine continued to grow as he recalls an influential third form teacher in New Zealand "who was really into wine and food and movies, got me into all of those things, and I started going to Film Society." By the time he had become a successful movie director in the 1980s, he and a group of friends had purchased land on Waiheke Island in New Zealand, home to world-renowned Stonyridge Vineyards. "But then the film business in New Zealand died," he explains, "so I moved to L.A. and got so much work there that I left it and sold the land."

During a visit to Phoenix to film a 1994 made-for-TV movie for Universal Television called *Knight Rider 2010*, Pillsbury met his future wife on the set and started spending more time in Arizona. "It was about a guy who smuggled immigrants by jumping a monster truck across the Rio Grande," recalls Pillsbury, "a pretty silly piece, but a huge amount of fun. We drove a monster truck through the Thomas Mall, which helped in its demolition, and they flew me from New Zealand to Phoenix, where I had never been." In Arizona, he found himself still holding on to his dream of a vineyard. He remembers a camping trip to Montezuma Well in Rimrock and watching the light of the setting sun illuminate the limestone cliffs. "I'd spent a lot of time in Europe with the movies," he says, "and I thought, that looks like Provence, we could do wine here.

Sam Pillsbury at his vineyard. *Christian Burns McBeth.*

The next day, I went for a walk along the creek and saw wild grapevines growing on the trees, *Vitis arizonica*, and thought, oh, limestone and high altitude—that's why grapes would grow here." After researching that part of the Verde Valley, however, he temporarily tabled his plan, finding the land expensive and the area rife with soil issues.

It turned out that a market in Scottsdale would guide him to the right spot. One day, he saw three Arizona wines displayed in a local grocery. "I think they were a Sonoita's Vineyard, a Callaghan and a Dos Cabezas, and I bought a bottle of each. That night I drank this '97 reserve Chardonnay from Dos Cabezas. I've been a Chard fan for twenty-five years, and I had never tasted anything like it. I found out Kent Callaghan made that from the Dos Cabezas Vineyard. I knew it was terroir, and I went down there and ended up buying land."

In 1999, following the trail of this remarkable wine led Pillsbury to Al Buhl and his vineyard. "I bought forty acres next to the vineyard this Chardonnay came from, and Al and I went into partnership." Pillsbury knew exactly what he wanted to do and planted twenty acres in a section called Norte with Rhone varieties, including Syrah, Mourvedre and Grenache vines. From the beginning, Pillsbury had a clear vision of the styles of wines he wanted to make. "From day one, I wanted to make an organic wine that came from one place, that honored that place, that didn't use stuff from outside. That was my thing; I'm a 'terroirist.' And I wanted to make food wines. I didn't want to make Robert Parker fruit bombs, which were all the rage at the time. So I wasn't doing something for marketing reasons. I did it because that's what I wanted to do."

His first wines were Diva, Roan Red and a rosé, and Pillsbury shares the story of why his rosés are now called One Night Stand. "Al and I planted grapes that we were told were Tempranillo," he recalls, "but that first crop wasn't. They looked like table grapes, but since we had a crew there, we picked it. Afterward, we pulled the vines out because we couldn't figure out what it was. Since we can never make it again, all our rosés became One Night Stand." At the time, Eric Glomski was making Pillsbury's wine at Page Springs Cellars. "It was kind of a weird wine, a slightly yellow, fruity wine," he remembers, "and Eric turned it into a pretty good rosé." That year, Pillsbury released his first three wines, and as he says, "I hit the ground running. Mark Tarbell [the *Arizona Republic* wine reviewer] gave me a ninety-three for the Roan Red and an eighty-nine for the rosé. And then someone from California said the Diva was the best wine in Arizona. I'll admit I knew I wanted to make a Provence-style rosé, but those grapes weren't my plan, so that was a lucky fluke. The Roan Red and the Diva, I knew exactly what I wanted to do. I wanted a Côtes du Rhône and I wanted a Châteauneuf, and that was what they were."

Pillsbury One Night Stand rosé. *Christian Burns McBeth.*

In the early years, Pillsbury made wine at Page Springs Cellars and, later, at the custom crush facility at Aridus when it opened in Willcox. In 2014, he procured a bank loan to open his own winery, which he did…in less than a month. He credits the assistance of James Callahan of Rune Wines with making it happen. "I'll love James forever for his ability to pull off shit like that." Although Pillsbury was hoping to have the winery ready for that year's harvest, he wouldn't begin construction until the loan was officially approved. As he tells the story, "The loan came through on July 8, so we literally started prepping the ground to pour the slab that day." Was he worried? "No, because I've made movies," he grins. "I was on my computer until ten o'clock every night ordering stuff. We pulled the equipment out of the Colibri Vineyard in the mountains that had been lying there for seven years. We picked an abandoned building up off the ground and reconstructed it. We bought old reefer truck trailers, cut their wheels off and put them on concrete foundations. We started prepping ground on July 8, and we were pressing Chardonnay on August 6…in a fully functioning winery."

Pillsbury credits having a firm objective and end goal as what brought him to where he is today. "I didn't go to grape-growing or winemaking school, and the same with film; I just worked with experienced people for a while. I've learned that it is more important to know exactly what it is you're trying to achieve, and then you can figure out how to get there."

CELLAR 433

With a total acreage under vine of close to 170, John McLoughlin of Cellar 433 owns the largest parcel of vineyard land in Arizona. Naturally, he is deeply ensconced in the viticulture industry and passionate about advancing education and recognition. In fact, McLoughlin was instrumental in submitting the application that resulted in Willcox being designated Arizona's second AVA in 2016. He describes the rigorous and time-consuming process that necessitated identifying boundaries and meeting the criteria that define a specific grape-growing region as having distinguishing features. "It took about three and a half years," he recounts. "You turn it in and they come back with a question, you turn it in and they have another question, and you go back and forth. You have to prove why your area is different than any other growing area in the world," he says. "Its soils, its diurnal swings, its temperature, its weather patterns. It's the true meaning of the word *terroir*.

It's everything put together that makes it special." The lengthy process involved studying topography and geography and hiring someone to draft the application. "But it's a great thing. It gives us legitimacy," he notes. "It says we're growing in a unique area and puts value on the product."

McLoughlin's story begins in his teens, when, as part of a bicycle racing team, he spent time abroad. "I went to Europe on a school program and as a fifteen-year-old kid was exposed to wines all over the world—French, German, Italian, Spanish, Portuguese, Czech Republic, Greece. It wasn't uncommon for several of us to open up a bottle and sit out along the Rhine or the Seine at a café and sip on wine like you'd sip on coffee." He remembers being most affected as a youth by the convivial bond of sharing a glass. "I just really, really enjoyed how wine enhances things, makes food taste better and encourages you to have conversation. It's social, it's communal, it's connecting."

Upon returning to the States, he worked in the restaurant business, and sampling with wine distributors heightened his appreciation. "I really enjoyed wine, and my enjoyment just grew," he says. After spending twenty-seven years in the insurance business, he felt it was time to adjust his focus, and in the late 1990s, he purchased a 320-acre property in Willcox, planting

Bitter Creek Winery at the Cellar 433 tasting room in Jerome. *Author's collection.*

his first grapes in 1998. "I just thought it would be fun to have something to do on the weekends," says McLoughlin, "where I didn't have to listen to people complain about their premiums."

His first 40 acres were planted with grapes including Primitivo, Viognier, Muscat, Gewürztraminer, Riesling and Mourvedre, and he now owns 400 acres of land with 170 acres under vine. "We've planted a lot of unique grapes and have a lot of stuff that nobody else does," says McLoughlin. "I just love exposing people to wine. I do this all the time. Someone will say, 'I drink Cabernet.' Then I'll say, 'You'll love this.' 'Hey, this is really good, this Cabernet is different.' Because it's not a Cabernet, it's a Montepulciano. I think people like styles over type, and I want people to experience wine they've never had before."

Due to the size of his acreage and labor costs, he switched to mechanical harvesting two years ago but continues to be a hands-on winemaker, something he feels passionately about. "I'm very opinionated about this," McLoughlin emphasizes. "If you ain't gettin' your hands dirty every day, all day, during harvest, you are not a winemaker. To me, a winemaker is doing the punch-downs and making the decisions. You're walking your field, you're deciding when to pick, you're running a forklift, you're working the

Winery 1912 at Vino Zona tasting room in Jerome. *Author's collection.*

de-stemmer, you're putting the grapes in the press, you're punching it down. You're integrated in the process. That, to me, is a winemaker."

With six labels in his portfolio—Jerome Winery, Arizona Angel, Bitter Creek, Sultry Cellars, Odyssey Cellars and Winery 1912—McLoughlin says he produces forty to sixty different wines in any given year. He's had a tasting room in Verde Valley in the mountainside town of Jerome since 2000 that carries Jerome Winery, Bitter Creek and Sultry Cellars, and he also runs the Winery 1912 tasting room in Sedona. "We're talking about doing one in Willcox," says McLoughlin. "We have a piece of property in the Kansas Settlement for a tasting room, but right now our energies are spread so thin."

McLoughlin has seen the region amassing more attention since the designation was bestowed. "Now that we're an AVA, we're seeing a huge influx of new people coming into the area. Of course, we have some growing pains that we're trying to get worked out as a Willcox industry, but you know, that's all part of creating a business. I've always said Willcox is going to explode one day. Realistically, 90 percent of the people in this wine movement were experts in something else. We could take all that expertise and create an industry that would rival Napa."

Lightning Ridge Cellars

"The one thing that absolutely stands out," recalls Ann Roncone of Lighting Ridge Cellars, "is a visit to Callaghan Vineyards. That was the 'aha' moment." In 2002, Roncone and her husband, Ron, found themselves making the journey from California to research the Sonoita area as they pursued their vineyard dream. Tasting wines made by Kent Callaghan reinforced their decision to plant new roots, literally and figuratively, in Arizona's southern wine country.

A San Francisco Bay Area native, Ann Roncone was a mechanical engineer in another life, but like many passionate wine-lovers-turned-makers, her vinifera hobby included home winemaking, classes at the University of California–Davis ("I took every course I could while I was still working") and summer vacations spent working at local wineries. "I was a cellar rat, and I learned a lot, and it just kept snowballing," she remembers. "Each year, I would buy a new barrel or another tank for my garage wine. And that's when it finally hit me. Wow, I really want to do this. Forget about engineering." With California's steep land prices, her husband's familiarity with the Tucson area as a graduate student at the University of Arizona and the lure of Arizona's first American Viticultural Area, their hunt brought them to Sonoita and Kent Callaghan's tasting room. "It was like, okay, this is very doable because this is great wine," recalls Roncone. "We made the leap, bought a parcel in 2004 and moved to Arizona." In 2005, Roncone planted their first grapes on the twenty-acre property, which included Montepulciano, Sangiovese, Cabernet, Sauvignon Blanc and Primitivo (Zinfandel). Why Italian varietals? "Back then, people were planting Rhone and Bordeaux varietals," Roncone explains. "My husband did some market research to see what was selling, and when the research came back, it was very predictable—Cabernet, Merlot, Chardonnay. The light bulb went on for me, and I thought, well, everybody does that, so I don't want to do that. I want to produce what I like to drink, which is Italian varietals. And then research turned to warm-weather Italian varietals, and it just took off from there."

The winery was established in 2005, their first harvest was in 2007 and the first releases debuted in 2009 with Sangiovese, Cabernet Sauvignon, Zinfandel and Nebbiolo. For a time, Roncone also cultivated a ten-acre property on Elgin Road, but "when we opened in 2009, I just couldn't take care of both vineyards and run a tasting room and keep it up the way I wanted to. We ended up shutting off the irrigation, pulling up stakes and pulling out the trellising so I could still use it." Roncone later sold the property to Phil and Kim Amundson, who also own a vineyard in the Uco Valley of Argentina and are now growing Malbec at Deep Sky Vineyard.

Roncone describes her winemaking style as "minimalist," with a focus on single varietals. "I don't want to steer the wine in a certain direction. I'm just guiding it along and letting it be itself." Currently, her wines are approximately 85 percent estate, with the remainder sourced from local vineyards such as Golden Rule and Carlson Creek. Nine varietals are now grown, with Roncone having pulled up some initial plantings like Sauvignon Blanc and adding others such as Malvasia Bianca and Muscat Canelli. "Montepulciano is our flagship wine," says Roncone. "I've had good luck with the Zin, the Aglianico seems to love it here, and I've had success with the Sangiovese as well. It was funny, because when I first planted everything, I wanted Sangiovese because that's more recognizable, but where I originally had the Sangiovese it was getting frost damage and I moved it. In the meantime, the Montepulciano and Aglianico took off. It was like, wait a minute, these guys love it here. I've

Spring in the vineyard. *Becky Limberg*

won a fair amount of awards for the Montepulciano, so, whatever it is about this area, it sure seems to like it."

Visit the tasting room villa and you'll drive by olive trees lining the driveway and outlining the bocce courts. In the last fifteen years, Roncone has observed increased visitors to her Italian-inspired tasting room. "There's still plenty of folks that come into the tasting room and it's kind of a head-scratcher for them—oh, wine in Arizona? But thankfully, Arizona wines have gained traction and taken off. The interest is growing in the people who are dedicated to it—because there's really nothing easy about growing grapes here—and with the dedication and the enthusiasm, it has a great path. A lot of folks have to try it for themselves first, but then they get that kind of 'wow' moment—oh, wow, okay, there's something happening here."

SAND-RECKONER VINEYARDS

For Sarah Hammelman of Sand-Reckoner Vineyards, who grew up in Denver, her love of wine began while studying psychology at the University of Colorado at Boulder and working in a European goods store. "The owner was German, and wine had been in his family for a long time," she shares. "He had friends that were sommeliers, restaurateurs and distributors, and all of a sudden I was surrounded by a different wine vocabulary and became fascinated." Upon graduation, she delayed a more conventional career to work for the 2006 harvest of Two Rivers Winery in Grand Junction, Colorado. She later joined the winery's marketing team and spent the 2007 harvest season at Etude Wines in California's Napa Valley.

Meanwhile, years before winemaker Rob Hammelman was to meet his future wife in Colorado, he had embarked on his own journey spurred on by a glass of Kent Callaghan's wine. A St. Louis native who studied at Colorado State University, Hammelman's wine interest was ignited while studying biology and fermentation and taking part in a wine-tasting class. After graduation, Hammelman moved to Arizona and was teaching math and science at a Phoenix charter school when he stopped in for a pie at Chris Bianco's award-winning Pizzeria Bianco. A glass of Dos Cabezas made by Callaghan inspired Hammelman to travel south, and that summer vacation found him pitching a tent in the Sonoita vineyard and working Callaghan's harvest of 2000. Three more years were spent teaching (and conducting further wine research)

Sarah and Rob Hammelman of Sand-Reckoner Vineyards. *Author's collection.*

Harvest season at Carlson Creek Vineyard. *Michelle Jonas courtesy of Carlson Creek Vineyard.*

Alcantara Vineyards in Cottonwood, Arizona. *Rhonni Moffitt.*

Deep Sky Vineyard in Elgin, Arizona. *Kevin Lewis.*

Every label of Rune Wines tells a story. *Kevin Lewis.*

The cooler air during night harvests maintains the grape's balance of acidity and sugar. *Jill Richards courtesy of Page Springs Cellars.*

Night harvest at Page Springs Cellars. *Jill Richards courtesy of Page Springs Cellars.*

Grapes go through a crusher/de-stemmer during harvest season. *Jill Richards courtesy of Page Springs Cellars.*

Wine tasting at Page Springs Cellars. *Jill Richards courtesy of Page Springs Cellars.*

Zarpara Vineyard at Grapes on the Grotto wine festival. *Author's collection.*

The bunker at Caduceus Cellars. *Michell Jonas.*

Left: Grapes at Keeling Schaefer Vineyards in Pearce. *Becky Limberg*.

Below: Spring in the Verde Valley brings flowering grapevines and fruit setting. *Becky Limberg*.

Right: Fall comes to
Keeling Schaefer
Vineyards. *Becky Limberg*

Below: A past season at
Canelo Hills, which is now
owned by Flying Leap
Vineyards. *Michell Jonas.*

Wine vats at the Southwest Wine Center. *Author's collection.*

Grapevines at D.A. Ranch. *Author's collection.*

The tasting room at Javelina Leap Winery. *Author's collection.*

The lodge and tasting room at D.A. Ranch. *Author's collection.*

Cabal Cellars tasting room in Jerome. *Author's collection.*

Véraison: when grapes begin to ripen and change color. *Author's collection.*

A seminar at the Arizona Vigneron Alliance Symposium at the Farm at South Mountain. *Becky Limberg.*

Owner Jim Graham and son Tyler of Golden Rule Vineyards. *Courtesy of Mike Pigford.*

Dan and Barbara Pierce of Bodega Pierce and Saeculum Cellars. *Courtesy of Mike Pigford.*

Tempranillo grapes at the Southwest Wine Center under bird netting. *Thomas Schumacher.*

Above: Dinner with winemaker Lisa Strid at Aridus. *Aridus Wine Company.*

Left: D.A. Ranch Red Barn Red. *Andrew Richard.*

Valerie and Daniel Wood of Heart Wood Cellars. *Becky Limberg.*

Brian and Megan Ruffentine of Garage-East. *Becky Limberg.*

Pillsbury farm-to-table wine dinner at Maya's Farm in Phoenix. *Christian Burns McBeth.*

Southwest Wine Center teaching vineyard in Clarkdale. *Christian Burns McBeth.*

D.A. Ranch in early spring. *Christian Burns McBeth.*

Volunteers and students at the Southwest Wine Center's annual "Plant-a-Vine" event. *Christian Burns McBeth.*

before he decided to leave Arizona to explore Colorado's wine industry. In Grand Junction, he worked at local wineries and was encouraged by a friend who had recently graduated from the renowned enology program at the University of Adelaide in Australia to apply. "Rob applied, got in and had a month or something like that to get to Australia," says Sarah. "It was a really cool international program working with people from all over the world." Armed with a graduate diploma in enology from the prestigious program, Rob returned to Colorado, and it is there, as winemaker at Two Rivers Winery and Chateau, where his and Sarah's paths would join.

In 2008, Rob accepted a harvest position at historic Château de Saint Cosme in Gigondas, and Sarah joined him on the journey to France. Spending time with winemaker Louis Barruol at Saint Cosme, an ancient estate on the site of a Gallo-Roman villa whose grape-growing history dates back to 1416, was an invaluable experience, says Sarah. "Louis is the fourteenth-generation winemaker in that family, and the cellar dates back to the Roman times. It's carved into a hillside in Gigondas, and in the parts that are used for barrel aging, you can still see the chisel marks. It has a remarkable history."

On their return to the States, they briefly spent time in Napa before Rob was once again beguiled by Arizona's unique wine regions. In June 2010, the Hammelmans closed on Peter Lechtenbohmer's Sweet Sunrise Vineyard in the Kansas Settlement area of Willcox. Because it had already been planted with three acres of vines—Nebbiolo, Syrah, two clones of Sangiovese, Zinfandel and Malvasia—they were able to harvest that first year. Their inaugural releases, the 2010 Malvasia and 2010 Nebbiolo rosé, immediately received widespread acclaim and restaurant placements. They have since added a half acre of Sagrantino and currently produce fifteen wines. In 2014, the Hammelmans started supplementing their harvest and now also source from nearby vineyards such as Rhumb Line, a forty-acre property at the foot of the Dos Cabezas Mountains Wilderness, and Greg Gonnerman's Chiricahua Ranch Vineyard, located on the Willcox Bench. The Sand-Reckoner label is a nod to Rob's science background and the calculations of winemaking (Sand-Reckoner is the classic work by Archimedes calculating the grains of sand that would fill the universe), but an authentic approach also defines their wines, some of which are foot crushed and all of which are hand pressed in their small winery. "We upgraded two years ago to pneumatic, so it's a little bit easier," says Sarah Hammelman, "but we're still hand pressing."

Sand-Reckoner Vineyards was the first winery to open a tasting room in Tucson, and the site in the Historic Warehouse Arts District is currently its sole location. There are plans on the horizon, however. "We want to develop something out at the vineyard over the next couple of years," says Hammelman. "We would really like people to see the vines and walk the rows. I'm also working with Native Seeds Search to grow native plants and vegetables and incorporate that into an experience for folks as well. We'd like to have a real hands-on experience and be able to hold workshops."

This authentic connection to the land is an important part of Sand-Reckoner Vineyards and was partly instilled by their time spent in France. "I think it was really crucial to coming to Arizona and making it work for us here," muses Hammelman. "The facilities that I've worked at in Colorado and in California were very modern, and Rob would tell you that Australia has a strong technical background, but Saint Cosme was an ancient, true old-world style. I think it kind of opened our eyes to a whole different world of winemaking. To listen to Louis speak about the wines and the land was just so inspiring—how he spoke about the way the fog moved down the river, the history and the terroir. I think we wouldn't have made our winery or take on the project in the way that we did if we hadn't had that experience. We just need the simple things, the essentials. We can build something and honor the grapes and honor the terroir, and it doesn't have to be shiny and new."

CARLSON CREEK VINEYARD

For Southern California native Robert Carlson III, his successful venture into Arizona winemaking with the founding of Carlson Creek Vineyard is a thriving family affair. His parents, Bob and Liz, travel from California to lend their support and often help in harvests and events; his sister Katherine is legal counsel; his brother John is the head winemaker and wine director; and he oversees day-to-day operations, including managing their three tasting rooms.

The career road he traveled took a roundabout route as he searched for a definitive profession, first with studies in aerospace engineering at Arizona State University, then art and finally political science with a minor in pre-law and economics. He interned for a congressman and was later recruited

John Carlson, Robert Carlson III and Bob Carlson of Carlson Creek Vineyard. *Michell Jonas.*

as a stockbroker, but there was another field that held an appeal. "Our family had been into farming for generations, in Poland, in Nebraska and in Minnesota on our mom's side," he explains. He recalls his grandfather's longing to return to farming and the many conversations with his father. "Our dad had talked about it for a really long time, but unfortunately, our grandfather passed away before it could be realized. And so our dad passed that on to us."

As a young wine enthusiast, he was familiar with Arizona's emerging industry. Carlson remembers early on being impressed with Kent Callaghan's wines and meeting Eric Glomski of Page Springs Cellars when Glomski hosted a private wine tasting for friends who were wine club members. The impetus to become part of the rapidly growing wine community was the defeat of a House bill that would have limited Arizona's small wineries' ability to sell their products directly to retailers and consumers.

"At the time," says Carlson, "I was working as a stockbroker, and when the laws in the state allowed for more direct sales, I saw an opportunity. I approached everyone with the idea, and we decided to do it as a family." After Carlson cashed in his 401K and John invested his college savings, with the rest of the family's personal and financial support, they spent a year looking at land in both Arizona's north and south wine-growing regions, deciding on a forty-acre property in Cochise County due in part to the low cost and success of the surrounding vineyards. "I found out how inexpensive land was in Willcox at the time and how good the grapes were," notes Carlson. In 2007, Carlson Creek Vineyard was incorporated and the initial forty-acre property was purchased. "Through 2008," Carlson recalls, "we did a lot of work. John and I were out there with backhoes—there were no structures, no well, nothing—and we cleared the land and sunk in a well." Their first vintage in 2008 was made from grapes grown at Arizona Stronghold Vineyards, now called the Al Buhl Memorial Vineyard, and their first vines were planted in 2009.

"Buying in Willcox was kind of a hedge," explains Carlson. "Because you're surrounded by other vineyards, you say, okay, I may not know 100 percent what I'm doing, but they seem to be doing good, so I'm going to plant here to be safe. And I think that's really how the Willcox Bench grew; a lot of people saying, if I plant next to these guys, I'm probably going to be okay." In 2009, the Carlsons planted their first varietals—six and a half acres of Syrah, Sauvignon Blanc and Riesling vines. "We picked Syrah because it was common knowledge that Rhone varietals do well," says Carlson. "The Sauvignon Blanc was a bit of a flyer. And the Riesling was because I had had one of Todd Bostock's dry Rieslings that was excellent, and it was made from Dos Cabezas Vineyard right down the road."

"When we got our liquor license," Carlson shares with a bemused smile, "John had to sign an affidavit that he wouldn't drink under age." Though he was not yet twenty-one, John Carlson was old enough to embark on an educational journey, and the brothers immersed themselves in the industry, taking viticulture courses at the University of California–Davis and surrounding themselves with experienced consultants and hands-on education. "We worked a lot with Peter Lechtenbohmer of Sweet Sunrise learning how to grow grapes early on," Carlson remembers. John also worked at Aridus Wine Company and later interned with Rob Hammelman. Meanwhile, Carlson was spending time up north in Verde Valley with vintners such as Barbara Predmore of Alcantara Vineyards and Rod Snapp of Javelina Leap Winery. "I also interned at Page Springs and was custom crushing," he shares as he recounts other winemakers he met during this formative time. "That was when Joe Bechard [Chateau Tumbleweed] was working as the winemaker under Eric, there was Corey Turnbull [Burning Tree Cellars] in the cellar, John Scarborough [Cellar Dwellers] and Sam [Pillsbury Wine Company] was making wine up there." First processing their wine at Page Springs Cellars and then Arizona Stronghold Vineyards, the Carlsons now make their wine at Aridus Wine Company, the largest custom crush facility in Arizona. "When Aridus launched in Willcox, we no longer had to travel five hours; they have state-of-the-art-facilities, and it's one of the nicest wineries in the state."

For John Carlson, it was a discussion with Rob Hammelman that he recalls as a pivotal moment in his education. "We were talking about Malvasia Bianca and the different ways to make it," he says. "It was kind of a cool moment for me, to realize that Arizona wine is not really bound by anything and can really be whatever it wants. I had never heard of Malvasia Bianca." "And now we have three and a half acres of it," his brother Robert interjects with a laugh. "It's kind of a cool thing," John agrees. "To know that because this region is new, we can define whatever we make as our own. That was my Arizona wine moment, just thinking about all the potential that this place has."

In recalling those early years, "the big fear for me at that time was that I'd have to go back to working as a stockbroker and I would feel like a failure," says Robert Carlson. "It took longer than expected, maybe six or seven years, before we reached any kind of profitability. Whenever we had any extra money, we would put it back into the vineyard and plant more vines." Over the years, they've purchased neighboring properties to fuel their growth into one of the largest vineyard properties in Arizona. The Carlsons added land to the south when the vineyard manager for Arizona Stronghold Vineyards moved back to the central coast and sold his property, and they later bought a 40-acre parcel to the east. "Then we had a neighbor behind us selling his 120, so that took us up to 240, and then we purchased 40 acres between us and Robbs Road."

"Our plan is to plant it all," Carlson continues. "Right now, we've got sixty acres under vine, but we're hoping to take that up to eighty this year. We're increasing our acreage of Malbec, Cabernet, Chardonnay and Sangiovese and adding Tempranillo. That Malbec completely took me by surprise. I planted it because of the similarities between Arizona and Argentina, and it has been a major producer for us. John wants to put in a four-acre blending block with different varietals, including Petite Verdot and Cabernet Franc. If there's something we like, we'll plant more of it." Beer is part of their future also, as the Carlsons have planted an acre of Cascade hops with plans for expansion in the next two years.

From the beginning, their strategy foresaw the ever-growing need for Arizona-grown grapes. "Even in 2006 and 2007, Arizona was still

Grapes in the vineyard. *Carlson Creek Vineyard.*

importing a large amount of grapes from California because there weren't enough grapes to fill demand," says Carlson. "Our plan is that we will always grow more grapes than we will personally need so that as the demand increases, we have the grapes. We modeled after what the Wentes [Wente Vineyards in California] do. Currently, we sell the majority of our crop, and last year we sold to ten different wineries. It's kind of a pay-it-forward thing. When we started out, though they didn't have a lot, wineries sold us their grapes and allowed us to use their facilities. I try to take care of everybody that took care of us and all the other people we contract with."

Now, Carlson Creek Vineyard counts fourteen employees, is constructing a seventeen-thousand-square-foot winery and tasting room and, with three tasting rooms located throughout the state, continues to introduce new fans to its award-winning wines. The original tasting room opened in downtown Willcox in 2010, a Scottsdale location opened in 2016 and in 2019 a third tasting room opened in Verde Valley's historic Old Town Cottonwood.

The two best-selling wines celebrate the family dynamics: the Rule of Three, a Grenache, Syrah and Mourvedre blend named in honor of Carlson and his two siblings, and Sweet Adeline Riesling, an homage to

Carlson's grandmother. "This has bound our family together in a way that I didn't expect," says Carlson. "I know many men and women my age who rarely talk to their parents, but I talk to my family on a daily basis and we run a business with them. We're taking the long-game vision on it and definitely doing it right. I mean, we'll probably see the industry where we want it when I'm an old man, but I'm okay with that. It's just good to have something in your hands that's representative of your family at the end of the day."

Chapter 5

The Chiricahua Foothills

Approximately thirty miles south of Willcox lies Pearce, Arizona, at the foothills of the Chiricahua Mountains. This southeast corner of the state is home to vineyards and wineries such LDV Winery, Keeling Schaefer Vineyards, Four Tails Vineyard, Aridus (a custom crush facility in Willcox that owns forty acres along Turkey Creek) and John and Karen Kovacs's Sándor Vineyards, which released its first vintage, Sándor's Rosé of Grenache, in 2016. Here, the soil is rich with rhyolite, a volcanic granite. As geology buff Cody Burkett observes on his website AZ Wine Monk:

> *The Chiricahua Foothills are a very different place from the rich, agricultural soils of the Willcox Bench which forms the heartland of the Willcox AVA. Here, the prehistoric paroxysms of ancient supervolcanic eruptions have provided an entirely different geology of eroded granites and tuff from the volcanoes, along with gneiss thrust up from the once-tortured earth.*

KEELING SCHAEFER VINEYARDS

"A lot of the characteristics of the wine made here comes from that rhyolite granite," notes Rod Keeling of Keeling Schaefer Vineyards. "The soil is just loaded with it down to several hundred feet because we're in the Turkey Creek Caldera. Sonoita in general has heavier soil with lots of clay and iron, the Willcox Bench is generally pretty sandy with some gravel, and our area is upland sandy loam and cobble."

Keeling and his wife, Jan Schaefer, were the first to discover the potential for grape growing in the Chiricahua foothills. At five thousand feet, their vineyard is located on a ranch on Rock Creek at the base of the mountains. They were originally drawn to the beauty of the area, and the initial eighteen acres purchased in 2000 were bought as a spot to build a home and not as a vineyard location. "When Jan and I started talking about having a vineyard estate," says Keeling, "we didn't think we'd be doing it in Arizona. We thought we were going to go to California. But once we owned the property, it evolved from there."

Keeling's pre-winemaker career spans professional pilot, traffic reporter and CEO of Tempe's Downtown Business Association, with twenty years working in downtown redevelopment and management. Now he and his wife own fifty acres in southern Arizona wine country, with twenty acres under vine. In 2019, they celebrated twenty-one years of wine production and Keeling Schaefer's fifteenth commercial vintage.

Keeling Schaefer Vineyards Rhone Blend Partners. *Andrew Richard.*

Though Keeling may not have come from a line of vintners, agriculture is in his blood and traces back to his grandfather Maynard Hill Montgomery, who grew cotton and alfalfa on a farm west of Casa Grande. "It's the 101st year of my family farming in Arizona," shares Keeling. "When my grandfather got here, he farmed in Gilbert, and there probably weren't twenty-five thousand people in Maricopa County. My brother's done the same thing. He's bought and sold farms in Casa Grande for forty-five years."

Like many, Rod's detour into the world of vinifera began with a glass of wine—in his case, Grgich Hills Zinfandel in 1994. "But I wasn't going to go out and buy a bunch of expensive wine to put in a cellar which I didn't have," says Keeling, "so I thought it would be more fun to try to make wine." Starting with home winemaking kits, he quickly realized grape concentrate wasn't producing the results that had inspired him and soon researched where to find locally grown grapes. In 1997, he found his answer at Dos Cabezas Vineyard in Willcox with Al Buhl. "I had talked to him on the phone, and I showed up at his vineyard," he recounts. "Frank DiChristofano was the winemaker at the time, and Kent was helping. I walked in and introduced myself, asked Al if I could buy some fruit and he said yeah." If Grgich Hill was the first wine that changed his perspective, he credits Kent Callaghan with introducing him to the potential of what could be made in Arizona. "I remember Kent opened his winery there on Elgin Road with a reception; his mother made all the food because she had a restaurant. We went in, and it was just packed; there was probably two hundred people in there. And we went through a vertical of his Buena Suerte cuvees, and it was all '80s, like '83, '84, '85. And that's really what got me thinking that Arizona could make high-quality wine."

For seven years through 2004, he would make the six-hour round trip from Tempe to Willcox every harvest season. "I would drive down and buy two hundred, three hundred pounds of grapes. We'd load them up in bins, drive to the Safeway in Willcox, throw a bunch of ice on top and drive home to Tempe. We'd go into the garage where we had a rigged-up deal to crush the fruit, and the neighbors would come over and help." In the meantime, they had started working on the property they purchased in 2000. In 2003, they built their first winery building with a small attached apartment, and in 2004, they planted the first eight acres. Their first commercial vintage was in 2005 with Two Reds Grenache and Three Sisters Syrah, which they still make today. Schaefer had retired in 2004 and Keeling in 2006, and in 2007, they sold their Tempe home and

Jan Schaefer of Keeling Schaefer Vineyards at Grapes on the Grotto. *Author's collection.*

moved to the winery site. "We actually moved into the little apartment in the winery," remembers Keeling, "and we lived there for a year and a half while we were building our house."

The couple also own nearby Rock Creek Vineyard. In 2007, they partnered with Roger Egan, the friend and restaurateur who introduced Keeler to that initial glass of Grgich, who has since retired. "We bought the lot when it was available, twenty acres on the same street that we're on. Well, I call it a street, but it's really a goat track," he chuckles. "Roger was a great partner. He taught me so much about business and how to make things work. I've been able to put together a great team with the help of my vineyard manager, Tony Rodriguez, who has been with me since 2004." All the wine at Keeling Schaefer is produced from the fruit of both vineyards, and in 2017, they opened a larger winery called Bodega Two.

Six grape varieties are grown on their fifty-acre property. Keeling recites the list of his vineyard fruit: nine acres of Syrah, six acres of Grenache, two acres of Mourvedre, two acres of Viognier, an acre of Picpoul Blanc and a half acre of Petite Sirah. "We're known for our big, ripe reds where we cold soak the grapes and extract the fruitiness," describes Keeler, though over the years as their winemaking has progressed, they've added lighter-bodied reds, whites and rosés. "In the last four or five years, I've backed the Grenache off and pick it earlier now, looking for a lighter body," continues Keeling. "We're changing our style on the big ones too. I used to go 100 percent new oak, and now they're 55 or 60 percent new oak. We evolve as we go forward. I'm trying to make wines for different people, and I'm pretty happy with the whites and the rosé too. We're not just about making big reds anymore, but that's really the flagship. We just bottled and labeled our '16 Home Place Reserve Syrah, and I had some the other day. It's only been in the bottle about five weeks, and it's just terrific."

LDV WINERY

Curt Dunham and Peggy Fiandaca of LDV Winery were bitten by the wine bug early but didn't necessarily think it would lead them to Arizona wine country. At the time, the couple were running a successful urban development business and, nearing their fifties, were pondering their next chapter. As they are avid cooks and wine collectors, their travels revolved around visiting wineries and bringing back special wines to add to their two-thousand-bottle wine cellar. "We'd look for the one down a dirt road that a local had recommended," says Peggy, "not the touristy ones. We'd go see this guy because we heard he's making an incredible Pinot Noir, sit at his picnic table in his backyard and drink his wine, then bring out a bottle when we entertain guests to share the winemaker's story. That's what fascinates us about small boutique wineries—finding those gems and the people that are passionate about what they're doing."

They can thank their friends Rod and Jan of Keeling Schaefer Vineyards for translating that love into a full-fledged career. Admittedly "wine snobs," they were in for a surprise one sunny afternoon when they visited Keeling and Schaefer at their beautiful Pearce vineyard property. Fiandaca relates the story of the couple they have called the winemaking pioneers of the region: "I've known Rod and Jan for almost forty years because I worked with them at the State of Arizona and heard that they had started a winery. We were familiar with the wine industry at that time, but we hadn't tasted a lot of it, and some of the wine that we had tasted was young or novelty wine and not…great." "You're being kind, Peggy," interjects Dunham with a laugh. But they jumped in their car and headed down south.

Kurt Dunham and Peggy Fiandaca of LDV Winery. *LDV Winery.*

"The first time I saw the area," remembers Dunham, "I thought to myself, this looks like Amedor County, California. I bet you can grow grapes here. Sure enough, we tasted their wine, they were good and showed such promise, and that's when our imaginations were piqued." Impressed by what they had seen, they were both engrossed in their own thoughts on the drive home. "By that time, we had been to so many wine regions, and visiting Rod and Jan and seeing how beautiful that area in the Chiricahua Mountains was, I thought, huh, this might be interesting," continues Fiandaca. "By the time we got to Tucson, we looked at each other and said, wow, there is potential here. Why don't we explore this idea."

They decided to return the next week and find a five-acre property for investment purposes. "We thought we would buy some raw land and maybe hold on to it and flip it as the wine industry took off in Arizona," says Fiandaca. "We found a realtor right away and spent the day looking at five-acre plots. And at the end of the day, the realtor said, 'I have this white elephant listing. It's more than what you're asking for and more than what you need, but will you just come look at it?' We said, 'Okay, sure. We have a little bit more time.'"

The "white elephant" turned out to be a beautiful forty-acre property in the Chiricahua foothills with a house and a large metal building used for heavy equipment storage. "Kurt likes to joke that he pulled up the driveway, saw this building on the property and it said 'just add grapes,'" Fiandaca says. Dunham agrees as he describes his initial reaction. "The building was just a shell, but all I saw was instant winery. The owner would wash off his equipment on a patio that we now use as a crush pad and then bring it inside. So the covered crush pad was facing east, which is what you'd want if you were building one custom, and it's just ideally situated. The guy didn't realize what a genius he was in building a winery," Dunham laughs.

"Once again, the property reminded me of Amador County, which is on the west slope of the Sierra Nevada," he continues. "It's so similar in altitude and mountain influence. There was a six-hundred-foot-wide creek with oak trees, and I was just enthralled with the visual appearance. And then to find out it had beautiful volcanic soils, it was just like, you've got to be kidding me. How did we stumble on this place?" Fiandaca adds that the property's home was also inviting. "It didn't look like much from the outside, but the interior had tall glass windows looking up at the Chiricahua Mountains. I said wow, this is really a nice house in the middle of nowhere, and we drove away intrigued and started negotiating right away."

An offer was made, the property was purchased in September 2007 and they celebrated Thanksgiving that year at the site of their future vineyard. By the following spring, they had two acres of vines in the ground, a process that usually takes much longer, and in 2009, they made their first wine. "We planted our first grapes in April the following year. Only about six months after we bought the property, we had sticks in the ground. It's pretty amazing," says Dunham. Serendipitously, a wine grape customer had defaulted on two thousand plants. "They were the exact root stock and exact grape varietal—Petite Sirah—that we needed," describes Fiandaca. "And we looked at each other and said, do we do it this fast? And can we do it this fast? Let's try it. That meant clearing the property and putting in the infrastructure and the irrigation from Thanksgiving to springtime when the plants would be delivered."

Dunham continues to marvel at the terroir of their happenstance discovery. "Our soil and the features of this property are very unique," he explains. "We're in a plume of volcanic debris from the Turkey Creek Caldera explosion millions of years ago. It's only about a half a mile wide, and that makes it very unique from a flavor profile, minerality and

The vineyard at LDV Winery in Pearce, Arizona. *LDV Winery.*

drainage, since the soil is very porous. Bass Creek, which is one of the main creeks that comes out of the Chiricahuas, is in the middle of our property and is a topographical feature from a drainage standpoint for both water and warm and cold air. The vegetation in the creek also really impacts the weather."

The location in the foothills of the Chiricahua also plays an integral part, including the all-important diurnal temperature shift. "The mountain provides another level of differentiation from most places," Dunham continues. "Because it rises five thousand feet above where we are, which is five thousand feet, that mountain actually creates the weather. It might be ninety-five degrees at eleven o'clock in the morning, but then we'll have a wind change and it will be in the sixties and the vineyard will smell like pine trees from the conifer forest at the top off the mountain. We might get two major temperature swings for that day, which is very unique."

LDV Vineyard has since added Syrah, Grenache and Viognier vines to its forty-acre estate. As Dunham explains, "We went with the Rhone varietals because we thought that they would do best in our soils and altitude, and being amateur chefs and interested in food and wine pairings, we wanted to plant grapes to fit more flavor profiles. We chose Syrah and Grenache because I love both of those grapes; Grenache is great with food, and it just made a lot of sense. We chose Viognier as our white grape because we thought it would do well in the climate, and it's very versatile. You can make it in a crisp, citrusy Sauvignon Blanc style or more tropical and completely different."

LDV Vineyards also ages its wine longer than some of its Arizona compatriots. "We get really intense fruit," says Dunham, "and we find that the longer we can keep them in the barrel, the more integrative and food friendly they become. With our last two vintages, we're averaging close to thirty-six months on our reds." They've also recently released a special limited-edition Rhone-style blend of Grenache, Petite Sirah and Syrah called Decade to celebrate the success of their award-winning wines and the ten years since their first grapes were planted.

For these globe-trotting wine collectors, sharing their story through their wines is what brings them joy. "That's our whole goal," says Fiandaca. "Nothing gives us more pleasure than like this last holiday season, getting texts and pictures all day long from people serving our wine at their Christmas dinner or on Christmas Eve. We want people to tell our story and to be excited about what we're doing and share it with their friends and family, the way we do it in our travels. It makes the hard work worthwhile."

Four Tails Vineyard

Barb Coons and her husband, Cale, are the owners of one of the newer wineries planting its roots in this rapidly growing region southeast of the Willcox AVA. Four Tails Vineyard is situated closer to the Cochise Stronghold and Dragoon Mountains in Pearce, and its name is a nod to the owners' first four pups: Bono, a basset hound; Dash, a skye terrier; and brothers Bubby and Bruno, golden Labrador retrievers. Thus, you'll find an image of Dash gracing a bottle of Short Temper Tempranillo and Bono memorialized on the label of Pretty Girl Viognier. "We had actually gotten Four Tails, LLC, earlier, not knowing exactly what we were going to do with it, and when the wine concept came into play, we said, oh, that's perfect," says Coons. "The whole concept of having a label per dog is something we've enjoyed developing. An amazing local Arizona artist sketches all of the artwork—she gets their personality—and Cale puts the labels together. He's also the mastermind of the wine leaf paw logo. People

Four Tails Vineyard's Amigos, their first estate Petite Verdot. *Andrew Richard.*

are drawn to it: 'Hey, we love dogs and we love wine.' Great, we're kind of banking on that," laughs Barb.

In 2013, the Coonses bought forty acres and launched Four Tails Vineyard on a family property. The couple, who live in Phoenix, had spent the last twenty years visiting the hobby cattle ranch owned by Cale's grandparents Lew and Alice McGuire. "As we were coming down here," Coons recalls, "we saw all the vineyards popping up and Cale's grandfather would always say, 'Hey, do you want to plant some grapes? It's supposed to be good out here.' Since we lived in Phoenix, it was just kind of in the back of our minds."

That changed after a visit to Verde Valley wine country. "Cale's grandparents had passed away, and the property hadn't sold," she continues. "We were in Cottonwood for some Arizona wine tasting, met Sam Pillsbury in his tasting room and somehow it came up that Cale's grandfather had property for sale. I blame Sam all the time because he said, 'You should buy and plant there. It's going to be easy; it'll be fun.' Sam still says to me, 'I don't think I said easy.' I tell him, 'I think you did,'" she laughs. "So Cale and I talked about it on the way home, and the next day we said, 'Are we really still thinking about this?' And that was the beginning of it all."

"Of course, we had a lot invested in the property from an emotional standpoint, and we thought, we're just going to give it a go," recalls Coons. "I think Cale understood what it was going to be more than I did because I remember thinking, did I just become a farmer? Cale likes to say, 'We sold a Corvette and bought a tractor.'" The Coonses, who also work full-time jobs, ordered vines before they closed on the house in April 2013 and by May had Cabernet Sauvignon in the ground. "We planted the first three hundred behind the house as a test plot. That was really a labor of love, putting those in and planting them by hand. And all the while we were doing renovations on the house since it was over twenty years old."

Early on, they had met winemaker James Callahan, now owner of Rune Wines, who became an indispensable guiding force. "When we first planted, James urged us to buy some local grapes to start our brand. He said, 'I'll make your wine and, you know, let's get you going.' And so we did." They introduced their first release, the 2013 Big Paw Syrah made by Callahan with grapes from Sam Pillsbury's vineyard. "He really helped jump-start us," says Coons. They continued to source Arizona grapes through 2015. "We asked James about grapes since it's cheaper to buy from California, and he said you shouldn't really because you're going to change your brand. If you start with California, the fruit is just going to be different. So we're very grateful for him for that advice too."

When it came time to expand their vineyard plot in 2014, Callahan was again an asset. "He helped us choose what kind of vines would be good here—what could blend and what could stand on their own," says Coons. His advice, along with a selection of personal favorites and what

Barb and Cale Coons of Four Tails Vineyard. *Courtesy of Mike Pigford.*

was available at the nursery, resulted in the current total of five acres of Cabernet Sauvignon, Petite Sirah, Petit Verdot, Tempranillo and Viognier. "We wanted to plant some Sangiovese, but we ended up with Tempranillo, which is actually great," shares Coons. "We are so excited that we planted that because it grows like gangbusters out here. That and the Viognier are the best-growing grapes that we have. If you come out here when we're in season, those are the biggest, craziest vines you'll ever see, and that has been consistent."

The year 2015 marked their first harvest from the initial Cabernet Sauvignon test plot behind the house. "I think we had three-quarters of a ton, maybe, which didn't even come out to twenty-five cases, but it was super exciting," remembers Coons. "It was Double Trouble, with our two labs on it," making their first release a 100 percent Cabernet Sauvignon wine made by James Callahan with Bubby and Bruno on the label.

Current vintages are made by winemaker Gary Kurtz (owner of Greater Than Wines), whose pedigree includes time spent in northern Arizona wine country at Page Springs Cellars and Passion Cellars and as an adjunct professor at Yavapai College teaching viticulture and plant biology. For the couple, passionate owners who balance their non-viticulture careers with their love of wine and the dramatic terroir of Arizona, there's a sense of pride and accomplishment. "We've done all of it. We put in the entire infrastructure for the whole vineyard, dug every hole and set up every line post, and actually, we're still married," laughs Coons. With winemaker Kurtz ("he's doing a fantastic job"), the Coonses continue to make 100 percent estate single varietals except for their Vineyard Pete rosé, which is a blend of all their red grapes, and in 2017, they upgraded their small "makeshift" winery to a full production facility.

"When you look around, this was the beginning of what Napa was a long time ago," says Coons. "We just need to make this a destination too."

Chapter 6

The Verde Valley

The conquistador stamps his feet, shaking off the fine veil of red-rock powder coating the worn, cracked leather. He squints into the bright sun as his gaze lingers on the river before reaching down to pluck a small, dusty purple-black grape from the surrounding vines. Burnishing the taut skin with a flick of his thumb, he pops it into his mouth: *"Este es el rio de las parras."*

While the exact circumstances are unknown, it's documented that in 1583, Spanish explorers bestowed the moniker of El Rio de las Parras (the River of Grapevines) on what is believed by most historians to be Beaver Creek in the Verde Valley of northern Arizona. Diego Perez de Luxan chronicled Antonio De Espejo's expedition in his translated journal *Expedition into New Mexico Made by Antonio De Espejo*, writing: "The river is surrounded by an abundance of grapevines, many walnuts and other trees. It is a warm land and there are parrots. The land is warm rather than cold. This river we named El Rio de las Parras."

These native grapes (*Vitis arizonica*), also known as canyon grapes, differ from European wine grapes (*Vitis vinifera*). Weaving their way over rocks, shrubs and trees, the vines bear small, thick-skinned black grapes that are tart and seedy. Existing historic accounts of wine made from canyon grapes in northern Arizona surround the mining boom in the 1800s, particularly around Prescott, which was then the capital of the Arizona Territory in the Old West. Resourceful winemakers and saloonkeepers slaked the thirst of prospectors, travelers and miners and advertised "fine wine" along with

The Arizona wine history display at the Sedona Heritage Museum. *Author's collection.*

spirits. As historian Erik Berg documents in his 2018 article "Equal Age for Age: The Growth, Death, and Rebirth of an Arizona Wine Industry, 1700–2000" in the *Journal of Arizona History*: "In popular culture, beer and whiskey are often portrayed as the drink of choice for miners and cowboys in the American West, but wine was popular as well and was often promoted by hotels and saloons as a mark of quality and distinction."

One of these resourceful businessmen was a Swiss baker-turned-prospector named Daniel Hatz who ran a Prescott hotel, saloon and bakery. An advertisement for his Pioneer Hotel & Restaurant in an 1881 *Weekly Arizona Miner* invited all to partake of the "Choicest Wines, Liquors, Cigars," while another edition mentions his "genuine native grape wine." It appears his winemaking career was short-lived, however, whether from California wine competition or the use of astringent canyon grapes, writes historian Erik Berg: "Even Hatz admitted that he had to dilute his wine with large amounts of water and then add 20 to 30 pounds of sugar per 40-gallon barrel before it was drinkable enough to bring to market."

HENRY SCHUERMAN'S RED ROCK WINE

Henry Schuerman. *The Sedona Heritage Museum.*

Enter a young German lad named Henry Schuerman. At the age of seventeen, in an effort to avoid conscription in the Kaiser's army, he left Germany and arrived in Quebec. He and another young man named Henrich Beinke made their way across the border and spent several years in St. Louis and New Orleans before parting ways. Around 1878, he arrived in Prescott and found employment as a baker at Hantz's establishment (where he was perhaps exposed to winemaking techniques), eventually running the hotel and purchasing it with his cousin George in 1884. In 1885, Schuerman sold his share to George and moved with his new bride, Dorette Titgemeyer, to a home on a 160-acre parcel of land in Red Rock he had purchased (or exchanged for a debt; accounts differ) in 1882.

Soon, he had established a large farm and ranch. The *Arizona Champion* of May 2, 1885, informed readers that "Mr. Shurman [*sic*], who formerly ran the Dan Hatz restaurant in Prescott, is now located on a ranch on Oak Creek, where he has cattle and other stock, also is raising grain and a fine garden." He had also planted over seventy acres of Zinfandel grapes, built a winery and began harvesting for his Red Rock Grape Wine. Local newspapers spoke of his "choice native wine" and mention "700 gallons of Zinfandel wine, which is pronounced first class." Great-grandson Larry Clemson, the family historian, shares the diary entry of family friends at that time:

> *Dumas Diary—Thursday, November 30, 1899: Clear and pleasant. Maggie and I went home from Schuerman's. He sent 43 bottles of wine with me to Prescott courier and Jerome miner. He gave me $2.00. I over paid him on fruit trees. Ollie went to dance at Camp Verde. Got postal card from sister at Phoenix.*

"His farm was known all over northern Arizona," says Clemson. "Everything I've read from the 1900s says it was a popular place to go, and they had picnics and big parties." He shares an anecdote about the famous writer and anthropologist Jesse Walter Fewkes: "He and his wife stayed with the Schuermans when he was on the property doing archaeological digs, and there's documentation in papers where he talks about their first-rate wine being some of the best he's ever tasted."

By the early 1900s, Schuerman's ranch and vineyard were well established, the winery's success due in part to the influx of workers for the nearby Jerome mines. Claire Jones, who worked on the property, told historian William Howard in his article "In Search of Sedona" that "in the fall, workers on the ranch would harvest 5,000 boxes of grapes. There were vineyards of considerable size—extending around the base of Schuerman Mountain." The March 5, 1914 *Williams News* included a notation that "pruning has begun in earnest on the large Sherman [*sic*] ranch in the red rock settlement. There are nearly a thousand large trees to prune aside from several thousand grapevines."

Although the first winery and home burned down in 1900 ("my grandpa and his brother Fritz were playing with matches," says Clemson), both were

The Schuerman winery and home that burned down in 1900. *Larry Clemson collection.*

rebuilt, including a larger winery made out of quarried red rock. But once again, the death knell was Arizona's 1914 amendment banning the sale or manufacture of alcohol. In 1917, Schuerman was caught selling the "last two barrels" of his famous Zinfandel and arrested. The December 16, 1917 edition of the *Prescott Journal-Miner* informed the public:

> *This is the tale of the harrowing fate of 100 gallons of good home-made wine. According to papers received at the office of the clerk of the Superior court yesterday from Justice of the Peace C.W. Bennett at Clarkdale, one Henry Schuerman, who has a well known ranch on the well known Oak Creek, did build a lot of wine, and did sell 100 gallons of it in two barrels to certain parties; also for $80. So, Henry was arrested, accused of selling vinous liquors, and was released on $500 bail. But this is not the end of the tale, nor of the wine. Comes now the authorities and report the case of Herb Thayer and Nola Dixon, who owned an automobile, and are alleged to have owned the wine as soon as they got through buying it from Schuerman. It is said that Dixon and Thayer transported the wine from the Schuerman ranch to the city of Clarkdale, where grief began to be stored up. The preliminary hearings were held and the trio bound over to await the action of the Superior court, the cases being handled separately.*

Although he was sentenced to six months in jail, due to his "exemplary conduct and good citizenship during a residence of forty years in Arizona," Schuerman was pardoned after paying a $300 fine. "I'm through," Schuerman asserted. "Never more will I transgress the law, even technically. Governor Campbell will have no reason to regret issuing me this pardon."

"They tried to get a cannery going around 1914 at the Crescent Moon Ranch," Clemson recalls. "I think they saw what was coming for their winemaking business and started buying the equipment, but it never happened." The mystery was possibly explained, Clemson surmises, when he discovered a January 14, 1916 *Coconino Sun* article referencing a heavy snowfall: "There were several buildings caved in. Among those we learned had fallen, were the buildings of the Oak Creek Canning company."

In the years following, the winery was lost to a flood in 1920. Fritz and Henry Jr., two of Schuerman's sons, took turns living on the homestead, and Fred Schuerman, a grandson, remembers the vineyard being replaced with a peach orchard by his stepfather, Albert Thompson. "The peaches became famous in their own right," says Clemson. The homestead was later passed on to youngest daughter Freida, and in 2018, it was signed over to the

Sedona Historical Society for restoration. Henry Schuerman passed away in 1920. Clemson's personal collection contains the following clipping: "He was a thrifty, hard-working man and soon had an orchard and vineyard that was the envy of all who saw it. He made wine for many years until the state went dry, after which he found a ready market for his grapes."

VERDE VALLEY REBIRTH

A Brooklyn native, William Staltari was the son of Joseph Staltari, an Italian immigrant who made wine in the basement of their New York home, a skill learned from generations of Calabrian patriarchs. In the 1970s, Staltari brought his family to Arizona and, after time spent in Tucson and Scottsdale, headed seventy-eight miles north of Phoenix, where he bought a twenty-two-and-a-half-acre parcel of land on Cherry Road by Cienega Creek. In a 2001 *Camp Verde Bugle* article, "San Dominique Winery: A Celebration of Flavors and Tradition," the writer notes:

> *In the late 1970s, Staltari moved to Arizona with his family with hopes of improved health for his asthmatic children. After several years of working in restaurants and in the insurance business, he decided to do what he knew best. He purchased a sizeable piece of land, began his vineyard and renewed the family tradition of making wine. "I got carried away with the romance of it. The whole idea of wine in Arizona is unique so I decided to do everything along those same lines."*

He tilled a plot located on a hill at 4,600 feet, planted his first grapes in 1977 and in 1981 San Dominique Winery was launched, making it the second of the post-Prohibition Arizona wineries to open its doors. Although initial plans included the small vineyard, due to water costs and weather challenges, Staltari soon moved to sourcing from local winegrowers. He was also an important member of the early winemaking industry, serving on the first board of the Arizona Wine Growers Association and playing an important role in the support of the Domestic Farm Winery Bill. Over the ensuing decades, Staltari expanded the scope of his portfolio, selling wines that included his 1980 reserve Cabernet Sauvignon and fruit wines such as Arizona Blush made with white grapes, plums and apricots. In later years, Staltari added a restaurant and specialty garlic shop before closing in 2017.

D.A. Ranch in Cornville is nestled in the heart of Verde Valley. *Author's collection.*

While Staltari is recognized as founding Arizona's first winery in the Camp Verde region, farther north, Jon Marcus is believed to have been the vintner pioneer in Oak Creek. "Larger than life" is a common refrain when describing Marcus, whose six-foot-five-inch stature fit his colorful background; he played football for the University of Michigan, was part of Dr. Kevorkian's defense team, bought the property after winning a lucrative lawsuit and it's rumored that he is now making rum in Puerto Rico. Marcus founded Echo Canyon Vineyards and Winery in a beautiful canyon on Oak Creek downstream from the McCain Ranch, having taken enology classes at UC Davis and spending time at Dos Cabezas in Willcox with Kent Callaghan. He purchased thirty-two acres in 1993, but it would be three more years before he made the move with his family, planting grapes and releasing his first wine in 2001. Along with the vineyard in Echo Canyon, Marcus at one point purchased eighty acres in Willcox (now owned by Bodega Pierce and Saeculum Cellars). Before he left the industry, future winemakers such as Eric Glomski and Rod Snapp would spend time gaining experience at Echo Canyon before moving on to their own independent ventures.

Following soon after, Ray Freitas and her husband, also named Ray, turned a residential neighborhood into a vineyard oasis. Originally planned as a fruit orchard, they found that the soil on their three-and-a-half-acre

Javelina Leap Winery. *Author's collection.*

property wasn't conducive to fruit trees. What to plant? As told to writer Steve Ayers in a 2011 issue of *AZ Wine Lifestyle*, "The notion that her land would support wine grapes came about in 1999 after a visit to John Marcus' Echo Canyon Vineyard." On March 4, 2000, the couple planted their first three hundred vines—Petite Sirah, Cabernet Sauvignon, Sangiovese, Merlot and Malvasia Bianca—on two and a half acres of their plot. Unfortunately, in 2005, Ray lost her husband to cancer, and the dream faltered. For some time, Ray produced wine with the aid of young winemaker Darin Evans. Today, Freitas still resides in her home with its backyard vineyard, which is leased by Alcantara Vineyards.

More people were inspired, and the next wave of Verde Valley wineries started to take root.

Deb Wahl was one of those earlier pioneers, purchasing a property in 2001 with Rod Snapp (who later founded a winery of his own) and planting four thousand vines on her portion to create Oak Creek Vineyard and Winery in 2002. In 2005, Bob and Barbara Predmore built their winery on what is currently an eighty-seven-acre tract at the junction of Verde River and Oak Creek and opened a Tuscan-themed tasting room at Alcantara Vineyards, the name a tribute to Barbara's grandmother. Rod

Snapp planted grapes on his part of the acreage he had purchased with Wahl and opened Javelina Leap Winery, harvesting his first grapes in 2005. He had previously spent four years with Jon Marcus at Echo Canyon and, while there, worked alongside assistant winemaker Eric Glomski before they both left to start their own pursuits.

In Cornville, D.A. Ranch is located on a beautiful one-hundred-year-old property that was once one of the largest cattle ranches in northern Arizona. In 2002, the Petznick family purchased the historic Verde Valley Dancing Apache Ranch on Page Springs Road, planting their first vines in 2006. Also in Cornville is Cove Mesa Vineyard, owned by Emil and Cindy Molin, former owners of an Oregon winery, who bought the property high atop a mesa in 2015. Emil Molin is a 2016 graduate of Yavapai College's enology program and is experimenting with lesser-known varieties such as Assyrtiko, Greco di Tufo and Teroldego. In Camp Verde, Ignacio Mesa of Clear Creek Vineyard and Winery purchased his property in 1999 and produced his first wines in 2004, and he and his wife, Sue, opened a tasting room in 2015. The vineyard is located in the valley of West Clear Creek at the base of the Mogollon Rim, and their Rio Claro wines are made exclusively with grapes grown on the property. North of Prescott in the town of Chino Valley lies Kit and Robin Hoult's Granite Creek Vineyards, built on a one-hundred-year-

Mae Rosé at D.A. Ranch in Cornville. *Author's collection.*

old homestead. The couple transitioned from growing table grapes to wine grapes and now produce wines such as Chardonnay, Syrah and Pinot Gris from a certified organic vineyard. In Paulden, Rick and Maricor Skladzien tend a six-acre vineyard located on the west bench overlooking Chino Valley at 4,550 feet above sea level. In 2009, they planted their first vines, with 2013 marking their first commercial crush of Pinot Noir and Carménère.

PAGE SPRINGS CELLARS

Like many people who follow a passion, for Eric Glomski, owner of Page Springs Cellars and Arizona Stronghold Vineyards, his voyage started with an epiphany. But it wasn't grapes that began this journey; it was apples.

Years before he founded his award-winning wineries, Glomski attended Prescott College to study riparian ecology, the science of ecologic zones adjacent to rivers and streams. "As I was doing research and projects, I would find abandoned homesteads because people settled along water sources," he explained. Invariably, there would be fruit trees and orchards on these neglected acres. "I'd show up in the middle of nowhere in the fall, and there would be these beautiful apples hanging from the trees," he remembers. During this period, he spent time with a friend and mentor, the famous textile artist Richard Landis, who was living in the Sierra Ancha Wilderness, a mountain range in central Arizona. "He was an artist, but he lived off the land there, had orchards, hunted and made his own wine," he continues. "Ultimately, he shared apple wines that he made, and he would say, 'It's all about the apples themselves.' I thought, well, I've been coming across all these heirloom apples in the middle of nowhere. How about I start? I would bring in an eighty-pound expedition backpack, pack it to the gills with apples, bring it out and start making apple wine.

"The moment I became a winemaker was when I made that first apple wine with pointers from Dick," he continues. "Almost a year later, I opened a bottle and the aroma hit my nose." He pauses as he remembers this formative experience. "And this is one of the most vivid memories in my life. My eyes were closed, and all of a sudden, I was transported. The essence of that wine somehow connected. And that was epiphanous for me because I had been a scientist up until then. Oh my God. This is an artistic expression of a place on the planet. It's a liquid landscape. You know, Monet paints a place and you look at it, you feel what that place is like visually. I realized, this isn't a

Gayle and Eric Glomski of Page Springs Cellars and Arizona Stronghold Vineyards. *Becky Limberg.*

visual medium, this is a different set of senses. And then I was pretty much possessed. I thought, I want to spend my life creating things like this."

The year was 1994, and he dived into his new hobby, knocking on people's doors to pick fruit and scouring the bargain bins at local grocery stores. "I was young, and I didn't have much money," Glomski explains. "I made blueberry wines. I made peach wines. I made apricot wines. I made banana wines. You name it, I tried to make something out of it. Some of them were horrid, but some of them were pretty darn good."

In the meantime, Glomski was teaching at Prescott College and had convinced Northern Arizona University to accept him to pursue graduate school working on a modeling system relating characteristics of river forests to restoration projects. During fall break, he was driving to California to volunteer during vineyard harvest season. These two interests would soon collide. "Lo and behold, the winery that I thought was making some of the best wine in California called me up and said, 'We were blown away by your work ethic from this last harvest. Would you like to work for us?' You've got to be kidding me. I had just busted my ass because Prescott College is pretty unconventional, and it wasn't easy for me to get into NAU. I had just convinced all these people that I was worthy, bending the rules everywhere. I felt like such a chump. And my major professor, Tom, a brilliant guy, wasn't happy, but he said, 'Eric, I've been watching you. It was clear that you had a parallel passion.'"

So in 1996, Glomski packed up his car, rented out his Prescott house and spent the next six years in the Santa Cruz mountains at David Bruce Winery, working his way up from cellar worker to co-winemaker. "To learn at David Bruce was an immense honor. I learned from some just absolutely brilliant and very unconventional people," says Glomski. "One of my mentors was Ken Foster. He had an amazing mind and an amazing palate and could figure out anything. Tony Craig was our enologist, had worked in theater and was brilliant in his own right. Our assistant winemaker, Lauren Tayerle, was a French horn player in the Berkeley Symphony Orchestra and conductor of De Anza Orchestra, and then Greg Stokes, the vineyard manager, was the real renaissance man. It was just this great group of people. Nobody was schooled in winemaking, but they were all brilliant and all loved wine and all were self-taught, and so they thought outside the box. It was just so cool."

To this day, Glomski can't imagine getting a better viticulture education. "I put my ego aside and I picked everybody's brains. I was like the Borg; I absorbed everything really quickly. I barely left the winery. Ken was like, dude, go get a life. I was like, no, this is awesome. I never want to leave, you know?"

But eventually he did, and in 2002, Glomski moved back to Arizona, where he would meet and marry his wife, Gayle. Serendipitously, he had connected with Jon Marcus at a conference in Sacramento six months prior, made a call and was offered a job as a winemaker at Echo Canyon Winery. It

Page Springs Cellars. *Jill Richards, courtesy of Page Springs Cellars.*

was there in 2003 that he met Maynard Keenan, who he would later partner with to form Arizona Stronghold Vineyards. "He was doing the same thing I did when I was talking to Kent Callaghan, which was going to pick the brains of people who are already there. I told him I'm going out on my own with Page Springs Cellars, why don't you start making your wines there."

With the financial backing of Glomski's family, Page Springs Cellars was founded in 2004, and Arizona Stronghold Vineyards was purchased in 2007 with Maynard Keenan. "At the time, all our projects were outgrowing Page Springs," says Glomski. "We were making other people's wines here too, like Carlson Creek and Pillsbury. So Maynard and I turned a facility that used to be a big furniture factory in Camp Verde into Arizona Stronghold Vineyards and moved Caduceus Cellars and Merkin over." After seven years working together, including the release of their documentary *Blood into Wine*, the duo parted ways in 2014, and Keenan took ownership of the Arizona Stronghold Vineyards vineyard in Willcox, renaming it the Al Buhl Memorial Vineyard.

Currently, Arizona Stronghold Vineyards' production facility is in Camp Verde with Bonita Springs Vineyard in Willcox and a tasting room in Cottonwood. For Glomski, being a good steward of the environment is crucial. At Page Springs, solar panels have been installed and a waste treatment system has been developed, and whenever possible, he strives to

Tour-De-Stronghold wine blending event at Page Springs Cellars. *Christian Burns McBeth.*

farm sustainably and organically. "For example, I have a river right here. If I dumped some nasty chemical in this vineyard and it ends up in that river, it kills the fish, it pollutes the waters that my kids swim in and it screws everybody downstream too. That's a different level of responsibility."

While their core wines are Rhone varieties and classic grape wines, Glomski continues to make fruit wines and brandy. "We make apple wines, we have pear wines, we have a little pineapple project going on and we're about to do a wine from Slide Rock up in Oak Creek Canyon." Mainstay wines like their signature Vino del Barrio and Barrio Blanca remain annual releases, but Glomski is always seeking out new varietals. "I've always been the type who likes a chalkboard menu at a restaurant, something fresh and interesting. We're working with Ugni Blanc, Nero d'Avola, Cunois, Cinsault. I've done different muscats. We've made things dry, we've made things off-dry, we've made dessert wines, we've done ice wine. It keeps us excited and our staff engaged. But we won't bottle it just because it's unique. It has to be great too."

With an eye to the future, Glomski also honors the past and is playing a unique role in continuing nineteenth-century winemaker Schuerman's legacy. In 2008, a local attorney named Stephen Schwartz obtained cuttings of the original grapevines from Sherman Loy, Schuerman's grandson. He planted them in his backyard in Sedona and asked Glomski to take a look.

When it came time for the first harvest, the grapes were delivered to Page Springs Cellars. "The amount was so small," remembers Glomski, "that we couldn't run them through our machinery, so my wife and I sat there, hand plucked all the grapes and made the first batch. We made five gallons of it. It was just a fun project. We bottled that, but then he sold that house, and we haven't heard from him since." Now years later, in partnership with the Sedona Historical Society and the current vines' owner, the vines have been rediscovered, and Glomski is tending the cuttings for grafting. Someday, Schuerman Zinfandel grapes will once again be grown and harvested at the original homestead, continuing the remarkable story of northern Arizona's historic winemaker.

CADUCEUS CELLARS

For Maynard James Keenan of Caduceus Cellars and Merkin Vineyards, his advent into the world of winemaking started with a dream—a literal dream.

In the mid-'90s, Keenan, a Grammy-winning musician who is the front man for the progressive rock bands Tool and Perfect Circle and creator of Puscifer, was looking to get out of Los Angeles and began to have a recurring dream about a mountainside town that seemed both welcoming and familiar. "In the dream," he remembers, "I knew it was supposed to be Arizona, but it didn't look anything like the Arizona that I had seen. A friend was in town visiting his family, and when I mentioned it, he said, 'I'll take you to a place where I used to live.' He took me to Jerome, and I was like 'Oh, that's it.'" As he shared in a column for *Phoenix New Times* titled "Why Arizona?":

> *As we entered the Verde Valley, my heart started to race. By the time we got to Jerome, I was vibrating. We—my inner dialogue and myself—knew this was the place. This was like that moment when you realize you've just met your soulmate. You just know. Your heart swells to four times its size. You are equal parts panic and relief. This feeling has never left me. This place continues to be an endlessly creative and inspirational crossroads for me.*

Like Keenan, whose pre–rock star youth includes being a gifted high school athlete and serving time in the army, and whose current interests encompass Brazilian jiu-jitsu and sketch comedy, Jerome possesses a unique and storied past. A historic mining town perched vertically on the side of Cleopatra

Hill, it's been called the "Wickedest Town in the West." It burned down three times in its history and even became a ghost town at one time. Today, it's an artist community, National Historic Landmark tourist destination and home to six tasting rooms: Passion Cellars/Salvatore Vineyards, Cabal Cellars, Cellar 433, Vino Zona and Keenan's Caduceus Cellars and Four Eight Wineworks.

Once Keenan was introduced to the haunting beauty and vistas of Jerome in 1995, "pretty much within a month I had moved." But winemaking was not yet a glimmer until one Arizona night a few years later. Sitting on the back porch of his home, Keenan watched as the moon illuminated the landscape. "I was drinking bottles that I had picked up on tour, looking at the slopes and remembering what it looked like in Spain, what it looked like in Italy," remembers Keenan, "and I thought, I should look into this."

Had he been exposed to Arizona wine before this vision of grapevines covering the slopes? "I didn't even know it existed," he says, but by 2002, Keenan had planted his first vines. "I started planting different grapes on different sites," he recalls. "The Marza block and the Augustina block initially had Grenache Noir, Sangiovese, a little bit of Syrah, Syrah Noir, and our Jerome initial planting was Cabernet, so we had a smattering of things."

At the same time, Tim White, current owner of Iniquus Cellars and Second Veil and founder of Kindred, who would later become co-winemaker at Keenan's Caduceus Cellars, was also following his vinifera path. Born in Pennsylvania, White grew up in North Carolina and, after visiting family in Virginia who introduced him to a local winery, moved to the region in 2003 to pursue winemaking. "I always found wine intriguing," he explains, "much more interesting to me than beer or spirits, but never thought about it as a career path until my sister invited me to a wine tasting. That was the moment. I thought, how the hell do you get into this?" After working as a cellar rat for four years, he felt a change of scenery was in order. Originally exploring options in Oregon, White answered an ad for Eric Glomski's Page Springs Cellars. In 2007, he started as assistant winemaker with Page Springs winemaker Joe Bechard (now of Chateau Tumbleweed), which is where he met Keenan. Keenan and Glomski were launching Arizona Stronghold Vineyards, and in 2008, White became head winemaker for their new venture.

In the early period of his research forays, Keenan had met Glomski, who was working as assistant winemaker at Jon Marcus's Echo Canyon Winery, and in 2003 he began making his wine as a custom crush client at Glomski's Page Springs Cellars before partnering to create Arizona Stronghold

Tim White and Maynard Keenan at Merkin Osteria. *Author's collection.*

Vineyards. Those early years of experimental grape-growing were a steep learning curve in Arizona's exigent climate, and Keenan's initial plantings for Caduceus Cellars succumbed to weather challenges. "Winter kill took out most of what was in the valley because we had no idea that we needed frost fans. First year, second year, third year and fourth year," he says in measured tones, and to produce his first vintages, Keenan sourced grapes from California. But he persevered, noting that grapes that have known struggle often produce the best results. "It looked like if we could get them to go, they were going to be good. Some of my favorite wines in Spain aren't where they grow the best, they're where they grow on the edge of disaster, and when they make it, they're the best of those wines. There's an edge down in the valley that's not the optimal place, but if I can do it, if I can pull it off, they'll be some very interesting, notable wines." In 2007, Keenan marked his first successful harvest with the release of his first vintage made entirely with grapes from his vineyard: Caduceus Cellars Nagual del Judith Cabernet Sauvignon, a loving tribute to his late mother, Judith Marie, whose ashes are spread across the east-facing slope.

In 2013, White left Arizona Stronghold Vineyards to pursue his own label, Iniquus, and it turned out to be fortuitous timing for Keenan. His wife, Jennifer, was running the lab and helping in the wine cellar, and the couple became pregnant in 2014. "At the same time, we were escalating production, I needed help and luckily Tim was available." With Keenan's travel schedule, White now oversees the wine production as co-winemaker, "and we've steadily increased production since then," he notes. But make no mistake—though Keenan spends time away on concert tours, he remains a hands-on winemaker. "There were quite a few times during the year from 2004 to 2008," notes Keenan, "that I just couldn't be there all the time. But starting in 2008, I came off the road for harvest. I don't tour during harvest times; I'm here on the forefront."

In 2015, Glomski and Keenan parted ways, with Keenan retaining the Arizona Stronghold Vineyards in Willcox, which he renamed Al Buhl's Memorial Vineyard. Currently, Keenan has forty acres under vine in northern Arizona and seventy acres in southern Arizona. "Northern Arizona is mainly Merkin," he explains, "and southern Arizona is mainly Caduceus Cellars. They do have crossovers and we do some cross blends. It makes sense when you're doing blending trials to add a little something here or there—a final spice that lifts the blend up or calms the blend down."

For Keenan and White, paramount to producing world-class wines is starting with the grapes. "I just think it's valuable for people to get out of their own way sometimes," says White. "Specifically, if you're trying to define a region, the more you should learn to get out of your way and not be a winemaker, but start from the ground up, the better. Obviously, a chef uses great ingredients, so ideally we use the best grapes that we can. You do that, and you're going to define the place and have integrity in the vineyard." Keenan nods his head in agreement. "Something we've found in the last couple of years," says Keenan, "is that there are all these interesting experiments we'd like to undertake—wild ferments, extended macerations, cold ferments. All those things are clever in the cellar, but we can't even begin to do those things if the grapes aren't coming in pristine from the vineyard."

"There are things that you have to get right in the vineyard," continues Keenan, "before you screw it up in the cellar. It has to come in pure. We're doing all kinds of experiments, but it's because Chris Turner, Jesse Noble and Juan Alba are growing fantastic grapes for us to try the experiments in the first place. You can't cut corners in the vineyard if you really want to see through a clear lens what Arizona is and what it has to offer." In keeping with that philosophy, Keenan explains why, as a musician, he's made it his priority to be home during harvest season. "You have to be present and in the moment to make the decisions. For example, we think we have two tons of Sagrantino coming in. Well, if that's the case, we're going to set up this submerged-cap

Caduceus Cellars 2014 Anubis. *Andrew Richard.*

tank with a 1.6-ton vessel and we'll have a bin next to it that will be a punch-down, open-top bin for that wine. You can say that, but then when it's picked, it ends up being more at 3.2 tons, or less and 1.6 tons. Those are production decisions that need to be made on the fly."

Keenan uses the analogy of a guitar player to emphasize his point. "That's your amp, that's your cabinet, that's your pedalboard and that's your guitar.

You wrote the song, so why are you going to go party and let somebody else play it and record it for you? You don't, because it doesn't work that way. The winemaker needs to be standing there, making those decisions as the grapes come in," says Keenan. "That's why you have to have somebody like Tim in the cellar who can also make those calls because we are aligned in our vision and purpose." Tim concurs, "We've been working together for quite a while, so all that goes pretty smoothly."

Keenan also credits vineyard manager Chris Turner for the role he plays in Keenan's ideals. "And then we have somebody like Chris," says Keenan, "who can say at the beginning of the season, this block generally tends to crop this much. Once we're through with shoot thinning and fruit set, he'll go through with a clicker to see how many we have. He'll look at historic records of average weight of clusters, average the clusters, count the clicks and we'll get within 15 percent of what he said. Everything ends up falling in place if it is that consistent. Knowledge is power, right? Fix the vineyard first, then go forward."

Ongoing education and the experience of those who have gone before him aid Keenan in his quest to define his vision. "There's a lot of people that have given me feedback over the last fifteen years. I always run things by Bobby Stuckey and Matt Mather at Frasca, as well as Luca Currado from Vietti, Taras Ochota from Ochota Barrels, Peter Gago from Penfolds. They're not going to sugarcoat anything for me. That's not in their best interest. Walking the vineyards with Taras, with Jason Barrette and Peter Gago, you really start to see how they're rating the vineyards that they're sourcing their fruit from and why they will pay more for that fruit."

Merkin Vineyards currently has ten labels, in addition to exclusive editions through the Velvet Slippers Club, and Caduceus Cellars approximately fifteen, with Four Eight Wineworks and Puscifer wines under the Caduceus label. Keenan's wine philosophy focuses on elegant, medium- to low-alcohol, food-friendly wines. "Some follow the model of the larger, score-driven, jammy California wines," he notes. "There's a lot of people doing that style, and I think as long as they're balanced, they're great wines, but the world has a lot of those, and I don't necessarily like that style. I'm trying to come in with the more restrained wines that will go better with food." He talks about wines like Nebbiolo, Barbaresco and Barolo. "They're not always a complete-picture wine. But you pour a glass with a plate of pasta, and it just comes to life. So those are the kinds of wines I'm making," says Keenan. "I'm trying to make wines that end up singing in the scenarios that you wouldn't expect them to."

FOUR EIGHT WINEWORKS

In 2013, the Four Eight Wineworks tasting room opened in Clarkdale, moving to its present location in Jerome in 2018.

Named in reference to Arizona as the forty-eighth state, Four Eight Wineworks is the brainchild of Maynard Keenan. An early supporter of the viticulture and enology program at Yavapai College, Keenan saw a need to help fledgling winemakers and graduates spread their wings. Though passion, motivation and enthusiasm aren't lacking, funds may be. The expense of equipment can be discouraging, and Keenan created a way to aid future winemakers in attaining their dreams by creating a co-op or alternating proprietorship where underfunded winemakers could have access to a facility to kickstart their production. "You see a lot of people who have talent, but they don't have the deep pockets or a loan for a facility of their own," he notes. "This alternating proprietorship is a place with their own bonded space to share, where they can use a press, a de-stemmer and all the equipment for bottling. They're making their own wine and growing or sourcing their own fruit; they just don't own the facility."

Four Eight Wineworks tasting room in Jerome. *Author's collection.*

Heart Wood Cellars. *Christian Burns McBeth.*

Interested winemakers submit an application and, if accepted, pay a fee based on amount of wine produced. All aspects of production are managed under Four Eight Wineworks, including transportation of grapes, administrative services and getting the bottles on the shelves in the tasting room and into consumers' glasses. "Right now," says Keenan, "we have six tenants: Oddity Wine Collective, Epicenter, Second Veil, Saeculum Cellars and Bodega Pierce and Heart Wood."

For Michael Pierce, the benefits of FourEight are twofold. As winemaker for his family's labels of Bodega Pierce and Saeculum Cellars, not only is he a tenant of Four Eight Wineworks ("he's close to leaving the nest to go out on his own," acknowledges Keenan), but as the director of enology at Yavapai College, he recognizes how invaluable this opportunity is for his new graduates. "Maynard built this incubator space because he saw the need for it, and there is a need, big time. It's so cost-prohibitive to have the capital and investment, especially right up front," he acknowledges. "If anything, we could use another one of that exact same model." And the model works. Chateau Tumbleweed is an inspirational example of what can be accomplished. "They were our first tenant," says Keenan, "and Joe [Bechard] and Kris [Pothier] basically ran the co-op. They graduated out, and Erin Center, his assistant, moved up to be the main facility manager and now has his own label, Epicenter. Chateau Tumbleweed has raised the bar."

The Oddity Wine Collective

When Chateau Tumbleweed moved out, it was an opportunity for Oddity Wine Collective to move in. For these three friends, meeting as students in the Viticulture and Enology Program at the Southwest Wine Center at Yavapai College was the impetus for the formation of the newest tenant at Four Eight Wineworks, and a passion for wine and shaping a new region was the unifying bond.

An Arizona native, Briana "Bree" Nation graduated with a degree in sustainability from Arizona State University with a goal of working in the wine industry. Her plan was to move to California, until she learned of the Yavapai College enology program and Verde Valley's growing wine region. "I came up here to scope it out with my best friend and fell in love with the area," relates Nation. "I thought, wow, these wines are awesome and this area is crazy. Sign me up! I guess I'm moving out of town." Aaron Weiss, who would become both Nation's business and romantic partner, was living in Prescott, having earned a degree in photography from Prescott College. He had registered for a business course at Yavapai College when he noticed a Wines of the World tasting class. That sounds fun, he thought. "I didn't realize that it was actually part of a bigger winemaking program," says Weiss. "I thought long and hard about it, and I said, you know what, I'm going to try something new. And it was fascinating. I couldn't get enough. I liked all aspects of it—the winemaking, the vineyard side. It just worked for me." David Baird had already enrolled in the college's wine program and remembers first meeting Weiss in the school's vineyard. His background in the hospitality industry includes time spent at L'Auberge de Sedona and in Jerome at the Asylum, where he credits Paula Woolsey, currently a wine educator and vice president of the Verde Valley Wine Consortium, for enhancing his wine appreciation.

Baird recalls early introductions to Arizona wine through Keeling Schaefer and Dos Cabezas, and as current manager of Four Eight Wineworks Tasting

Sacculum Cellars One Stone and Oddity Wine Collective Darwin's Dilemma. *Author's collection.*

Room, he was the conduit for the group to join the co-op. Nation begins with the story. "Maynard and Nikki [Check] were on *Good Morning America*, and Maynard said he was opening this alternating proprietorship facility and wanted to offer one of the first top graduates from the program a spot on Four Eight." "In the meantime," Weiss continues, "I had already started working for Dave in the tasting room and was one of the first top graduates. Then Tumbleweed had their success and was talking about moving out, so the conversation came up with who's going to be next?"

Baird continues: "After learning that Tumbleweed was no longer producing with us, I asked Maynard, 'What happens when 25 percent of my stock leaves? What's the plan?' And his answer was, 'Well, you do it. Aaron's the dude that we gave this shoe-in for, you guys have the education, you know what you're doing, so just do it.' At that point I went through this crazy existential panic moment of, wait, that's not what I'm planning on doing; I was just trying to run a tasting room. But I called Bree and Aaron, and we sat down at the 10/12 Lounge and put together a plan. We became incorporated in 2014 and had our first vintage in 2015."

It's a symbiotic relationship that runs smoothly says Weiss. "We're all friends, but the fact is that it has worked out in our different roles. For me,

I see numbers of any kind and smoke comes out of my ears. There's the chemistry component of winemaking, and Bree geeks out about it. And then Dave has more business experience than any of us. We all help each other out with everything. If I need help in the winery, I just have to say, hey guys, I need some extra hands. It's a partnership that just works out." All their fruit is sourced from Willcox, "except," says Nation, "a really small amount of Zin that we helped farm in a backyard vineyard in Sedona, and that was a lot of fun."

A collaborative incubator has turned into the ideal platform for this innovative and clever team. Baird shares the development of their distinctive intertwined vine logo, starting with his wife shaping the copper wiring from a paperweight to form an *O*, *W* and *C*. They were just as resourceful with their unique screen-printed bottles. With such a small production, it wasn't feasible to pay for paper labels for their lot of bottles. "It was 100 percent out of necessity," says Baird. "Our production was so small that we couldn't hit the minimum requirements for these label companies within a price point that would work, so we found someone in Phoenix that prints growlers. We order our bottles through the same company that everybody else uses, but he screen-prints them for us. We were the first wine bottles he's ever done. So we actually were able to minimize our costs using somebody local and at the same time elevate our presence and our look. You have to utilize your resources and your connections."

This principle has translated into their wine philosophy, exemplified by the impressive debut of a wine called Unsanctioned. In sharing his thoughts on what defines the Arizona vintner, Cody Burkett, founder of AZ Wine Monk, speaks of Oddity's esoteric release. "I think a renegade is something that is a definite character not only of Arizona winemakers, but of Arizona wine in general, because we're not necessarily going to follow the traditions of other places. Look at Oddity, who made a Petite Sirah and Sangiovese blend called Unsanctioned. Who does that? And it's beautiful! Who would think to blend Sangiovese and Petite Sirah? Arizona winemakers, the renegades."

Again, this creativity stems from the team's skill and a spirit of resourcefulness. "Arizona hasn't defined what its grapes are," says Weiss, "but Oddity has embraced that, partly since we're the smallest kids on the block. We don't always get the pick of the grapes that we want, so we're rolling with it and riding the wave." Using this for inspiration, they've orchestrated blind tasting sessions with friends and family. "That's the way we came up with Unsanctioned," Weiss explains, "which is a really obscure blend. We did all of our tastings blind, and instead of having blends that we're trying to make, we

Aaron Weiss of the Oddity Wine Collective. *Becky Limberg.*

came up with as many blends that will work with the volumes that we have that won't leave us with a half barrel somewhere. We did a blind vote and came up with the Unsanctioned. I remember, we read it and we were like, really? So we're going to do a 50:50 Sangio and Petite Sirah blend? Really? And people love it. It was because we put our faith in our palates, not the marketing."

Baird agrees. "The market drives so many decisions of winemakers. In my experience, I find that Arizona wines can be super fruit-forward or they can be really hot with high alcohol. Our goal is an evolution within the palate, and so you'll find with our wines that you'll get this nice kind of fruit pop, there's a mid-palate conversation and then it finishes leaving you wanting a little bit more. You do taste our climate, you do taste our terroir, but we have the luxury, since we're a co-op with the three of us, of babying our wines, doing slower ferments and really walking it through. It's more of an old-world European-style wine, which I think Arizona is so ripe for. Because we're dealing with a co-op and don't have the crazy overhead that other wineries do, we can really take the time to do it slowly and do it properly. I know that when we're out on our own, that's going to be our philosophy."

"Ten years ago," Weiss recalls, "I had no idea what was going on in Arizona wine country until I went to a friend's birthday party where he had a wine tasting. Looking back on it, it's really embarrassing. And once I went back to school for winemaking, I went into my dad's wine cellar, and there's an empty 2000 or 2002 bottle of Callaghan wine on his shelf. He liked it well enough to save the bottle. I mean, this is a wine cellar full of Margaux! Now we're the ones making Arizona wine," says Weiss. "And he's buying it," interjects Baird. "He's our number-one fan," adds Nation with a laugh.

"I think the truest ode to Arizona is that we're doing whatever we want," muses Baird. "Because what is Arizona wine? One of my good friends who works at Page Springs Cellars was telling her husband, 'I don't understand why they call themselves the Oddity Wine Collective; they're all really normal people.' And that's a great thing. Because it's not about us. It's that by naming ourselves the Oddity Wine Collective, we relinquish any handcuffs that could come with expectations. You can't expect anything from Oddity Wine Collective, because they're collectively doing what they want to do."

"When they moved on, Tumbleweed legitimized Four Eight Wineworks," notes Baird. And then that created a space for Oddity Wine Collective. We stepped up to the plate, and that's where we're at now until we move on. It's because of Yavapai College. It's because of Aaron and Bree. It's because of Chateau Tumbleweed. It's because of Four Eight Wineworks and Maynard. All these people who took a chance on us."

Maynard Keenan likewise recognizes that Four Eight Wineworks is accomplishing its purpose. "Like anything, there's so many moving parts and personalities that it's hard to completely dial it in, but I think we've done a pretty good job. It's just comfortable enough to where if you want to be in that setting and it's working out like you thought it would, then great, then you're going to go out and conquer the world. Perfect. That's what Chateau Tumbleweed did; they went out and started their own thing. And if you kick ass, we'll all follow."

CHATEAU TUMBLEWEED

Pick up a bottle of Chateau Tumbleweed, and your eye is immediately drawn to the quirky figures with visages replaced by tumbleweeds, designed to capture the individuality of the wines and the spirit of the owners. While Kris Pothier handles sales and is the artist behind the beloved unconventional labels, the remainder of the two couples who make up the team all play their intrinsic roles: her husband, Joe Bechard, is the winemaker; Kim Koistinen handles administration and accounting; and Jeff Hendricks takes care of design aspects and fruit sourcing. Flip the bottle around, and you'll find wine specs on the back label such as vintage designation, varietal composition, appellation and detailed sugar, acid and pH levels, borne out of frustration, says Pothier, at the lack of information they've found on bottles in the course of their wine research. To come up with the name of their winery, the quartet brainstormed some "silly stuff" fueled by wine and lasagna in the White Mountains and settled on Chateau Tumbleweed as representing how they "all blew into town" before converging to plant their roots in the Verde Valley.

Seated in their cozy and inviting Clarkdale tasting room, Pothier and Bechard gesture at the surroundings. "We wanted to avoid a sterile, pretentious kind of feeling," says Bechard, and Pothier agrees. "We really wanted it to reflect who we are," she says, "which in turn has given us a really cool group of people that come here all the time." Launched in 2015, they've already outgrown the space in the three successful years since they opened their doors.

Their wine story starts in Eugene, Oregon, while Bechard was attending the University of Oregon Journalism School. "We worked at a restaurant where a lady had a lot of good wine and was pretty open about sharing," he recalls. "That's where we fell in love with wine, and I ended up turning a lot

Chateau Tumbleweed. *Andrew Richard.*

of my school assignments into stories about wine. But I had no interest in getting into the business at all, no idea that one could even do that." After graduating, Bechard took a job at *Sedona Red Rock News*, and they moved to Arizona "sight unseen," little knowing that the wind was to soon blow these tumbleweeds in another direction.

It was while working for the newspaper that Bechard first heard of Page Springs Cellars. "I had a pretty big beat at the paper, and I was really blown away to hear that there was somebody making wine in Arizona," he says. "The two main guys at that time were Eric Glomski and Jon Marcus at Echo Canyon. I think at that time there were only nine bonded wineries." He featured the pair in his stories, but after a year at the newspaper, he decided it was time for a change. "I was kind of disenchanted with community journalism and quit my job before I had any real plan," he says. "But I went straight to Eric and said, hey man, I need something to do, and was hired for the harvest of 2005. I did fifty tons my first harvest, which is actually what we're doing here right now." Glomski and Keenan were soon to open Arizona Stronghold Vineyards, and Bechard's part-time harvest job stretched into five years as winemaker for Page Springs Cellars, where he recalls helping Ray Freitas with racking and blending when she lost her husband. In the interim, Pothier attended film school and, upon graduating, at one point worked as an assistant for Sam Pillsbury. "It was a fun time," she says. "I slept in a back room with cases of wine around me."

The couples behind Chateau Tumbleweed all got their start at Page Springs Cellars, with Pothier as the first tasting room attendant in 2004, and later Bechard, Koistinen, Hendricks and Pothier all worked in the cellar. In 2010, Bechard left Page Springs. "I actually sent two resumes out to California, and we debated moving somewhere else because there weren't a lot of jobs here at that time, especially winemaker jobs. How do we stay in Arizona? Rod Snapp kind of saved me and gave me a job with the 2010 harvest." Around this time, the four friends had begun talking about starting their own label. "We were hanging out, sitting around the table, drinking wine and talking about how we could get into the industry," says Bechard. "We all had experience in different aspects, so we thought we could make a good team." Bechard found a position as winemaker at Alcantara Vineyards, and that proved to be a momentous decision for another reason: "We ended up buying three barrels of Merlot from Barbara, and that was when Chateau Tumbleweed was born." In 2011, while Bechard was at Alcantara Vineyards, Maynard Keenan approached him with his idea for the Four Eight Wineworks co-op. "We were still aging our barrels, and we weren't sure what we were going to do. We barely had any money, but we said, you know, let's give it a shot." "At this point we were already business partners with Kim and Jeff," Pothier adds, "and Jeff had worked with Maynard and Chris Turner in the vineyards."

"We were kind of the guinea pigs," says Bechard, "to test the concept and the facility in Camp Verde. It gave Chateau Tumbleweed real room to grow because Barbara didn't have the space for us to be making wine there." One challenge to overcome was a law prohibiting more than one winery to operate at a single production facility. "Everyone thought we were crazy because they didn't understand what we were talking about," remembers Pothier. Legislation was passed to allow alternating proprietorships in 2014, but until then, their wines had to be distributed under the Caduceus Cellars license. During that time, the couple balanced dual jobs—Bechard making wine for Chateau Tumbleweed while acting as manager of the co-op, and Pothier handling shipping and national sales for Caduceus Cellars and Merkin, along with marketing for Chateau Tumbleweed's label. Their first vintage was just under three hundred cases of the 2011 Merlot barreled at Alcantara Vineyards. In 2012, they made five hundred cases, and in 2013, they produced one thousand cases. With experience gained at Four Eight Wineworks over those years, they were ready to spread their wings and had started to look for their own facility, eyeing a building in Clarkdale on AZ-89A that Pothier would pass while delivering wines to Jerome. Finances, however, were still an issue. "The four of us went to the bank, but we couldn't get

Kris Pothier and Joe Bechard of Chateau Tumbleweed. *Becky Limberg.*

a loan for the location because we didn't have enough sales," Pothier recalls. "But I kept the dream alive somewhere in my little pocket because we had it all spelled out, we were ready to do it, but the bank was like, no, not yet. But we were so ready."

Little did they know that another providential opportunity was brewing. The group had met Earl and Melinda Petznick of DA Ranch early on when they were making wine at AZ Stronghold. The Petznicks, who operate one of the largest privately-owned agricultural businesses in Arizona, had grown from making wine as a family hobby to a full-fledged business and were looking for a new winemaking proposition. "It's what everyone looks for, and it came to us," says Pothier gratefully. "We were super lucky; they're really great." With the Petznicks' help, the building was bought and renovated ("it used to be a guy's really fancy man cave, so we ripped out the bedrooms and kitchen and finished it in four months," says Pothier) for their winery's grand opening in July 2015.

"A lot of people think we just came out of nowhere, but we had a long history with two vintages stockpiled by the time we launched this place," says Pothier. With their wines garnering awards and Chateau Tumbleweed playing its role in the establishment of northern Arizona's wine region, both acknowledge it's an inspiring time. "The attitude has changed so much in the last five years," says Bechard. "It's exciting to be here."

THE TASTING ROOMS OF COTTONWOOD

The popular Verde Valley Wine Trail and associated public art exhibit Painted Barrels on the Verde Valley Wine Trail are part of a targeted effort to promote the industry and introduce visitors and locals alike to this thriving wine region. "The economic impact of the wine industry on the Verde Valley is substantial," says Tom Schumacher, president of the Verde Valley Wine Consortium. "We actually did two different studies, Northern Arizona University and the University of Arizona, that showed the economic value and impact from the wine industry and how it's changed over the years. It's significant. One thing that has really helped is the Verde Valley Wine Trail." The Wine Trail campaign launched in 2009 and maps a collection of tasting rooms and wineries that are scattered throughout the towns of Cornville, Cottonwood, Clarkdale, Jerome, Sedona and other parts of the Verde Valley. Presently, there are

Gallifant Cellars at Winery 101 in Cottonwood. *Author's collection.*

twenty-four wineries and tasting rooms, six of which are located within walking distance to each other in Cottonwood, which touts itself as "the heart of Arizona wine country."

The first two tasting rooms to open their doors and usher in a new era were Arizona Stronghold Vineyards and Pillsbury Wine Company in 2009. Sam Pillsbury recalls the early days. "Ten years ago, I said to Eric Glomski, I need a tasting room, and he said, 'We need a tasting room for Stronghold.' Because it was on the Verde Valley Wine Trail, we looked at Cottonwood, but at the time, most of the shops were shuttered. But just look at it now." He credits not only intuitive thinking and a smart decision to help jump-start what was once a sleepy historic town but also the support of the local council and community. "From day one in Cottonwood, they were behind this," says Pillsbury. "They were good about helping us, and look what's happened." Now wineries from both northern and southern Arizona are pouring their wares in Old Town Cottonwood, which has also seen a symbiotic boom in hotels and restaurants. "It's pretty amazing how different the downtown area is now," says Tom Schumacher. "It's such a wonderful place to come up for a weekend or for a few days. I tell people, come to Old Town, park your car and walk for the weekend. You can go to nice restaurants, different tasting rooms, walk down by the river, and there's hiking nearby."

In addition to Pillsbury and Arizona Stronghold Vineyards tasting rooms, guests can stroll along Main Street to visit Winery 101, home to Gallifant Cellars and Southpaw Cellars, as well as Carlson Creek Vineyards, which opened its third tasting room in 2019. At Merkin Tasting Room and Osteria, a full-service restaurant, Chef Christopher Smith makes fresh pasta and bakes bread in-house with a menu offering fresh ingredients harvested from Maynard Keenan's orchards and gardens to pair with the selection of wines.

At Burning Tree Cellars, Mitch Levy runs the day-to-day operations while Corey Turnbull is in charge of winemaking. Like many, Mitch Levy has a multifaceted past, which includes former chef, paramedic, military man and a career in finance. A longtime fan of Page Springs Cellars as an Inner Circle wine club member, Levy's next career led him to the wine industry. "I retired from running a finance company when I met Corey," he says. "One thing led to another, and we started Burning Tree. I left a job making six figures a year to do this. It was always something I wanted to do."

Corey Turnbull and Mitch Levy of Burning Tree Cellars. *Becky Limberg.*

Currently making their wine at Arizona Stronghold Vineyards and Page Springs Cellars, Levy shares that they are in the process of looking for a spot to build their own winery. Their first wine, the Lotus, was produced in 2007, and Burning Tree Cellars now offers approximately twenty different wines, serving four flights of five at its tasting room.

"We do a lot of Rhone-style wines, and most have won gold and silver medals," says Levy. "We like to let the grape dictate how the wines are expressed and want to be a small-batch boutique winery that a lot of people know about." He's happy to see the growth over the last decade. "We as a community have accomplished a lot in the little bit of time that we've been around. Give us another ten or fifteen years and I think Arizona is going to surprise a lot of people."

Chapter 7

Arizona Wine Looks to the Future

There's no mistaking that Arizona's wine industry is flourishing and displaying exponential growth far more quickly than what was predicted even just ten years ago. The industry's renaissance has made immense strides in the few decades since its rebirth, and Arizona's climate and topography offer a unique advantage to the vineyards that dot its landscape. Its presence has been strengthened in both the national and international arena as winemakers continue to be recognized and awarded, breaking the barrier of misguided expectations and validating the quality of the wines being produced in Arizona. "We're only going to get better," says advanced sommelier Jason Caballero, wine director at Scottsdale's Maple & Ash and a mentor to young sommeliers. "Everybody's working hard. They're putting in the work. They're pooling their resources. They're acting like a world-class wine region, and we're going to attain that status."

Wine production in the state continues to climb and each year ushers in significant advancements in viticulture practices and winemaking techniques. In 2005, there were nine bonded wineries. Today, the Grand Canyon State boasts over one hundred. One attraction is the cost of land, which is less expensive than in California or other major wine states. "One of the great things about Arizona wine," acknowledges Robert Carlson, "is there is a lower barrier to entry here than the more established wine-growing regions. Land is cheaper and we have a climate that is conducive to agriculture." According to the 2017 Arizona Wine Tourism Industry report, the industry created an estimated $56,178,643 in total economic output, 640.6 full-time

The vineyard at Southwest Wine Center at Yavapai College. *Author's collection.*

equivalent jobs and approximately $3.6 million in local and state taxes generated from Arizona wine tourism expenditures. "Arizona wine is just getting better," says Kent Callaghan. "No question. There's better viticulture. There's better winemaking. Yavapai College is helping with that."

YAVAPAI COLLEGE

Tom Schumacher, art professor and campus administrator of Yavapai College, is sitting in his office at the Verde Valley campus overlooking the vineyard that was planted by Maynard Keenan in Clarkdale as part of Arizona's only enology and viticulture program. "I wanted it to be very visible so visitors know it's here," says Schumacher. "It's a beautiful location right in the foothills where people can see the red rocks off in the distance."

Schumacher is also in his sixth year as president of the Verde Valley Wine Consortium, a coalition formed to promote the Verde Valley as a significant wine region. "It is certainly the up-and-coming wine location in Arizona," he notes. "Most of the Verde Valley is at the 3,500- to 4,000-foot level, so it's the high desert but perfect for growing grapes as well." In 2017, the consortium submitted an application to recognize the Verde Valley as the newest American Viticulture Area with at that time twenty-two vineyards and approximately 125 acres under vine. Currently, the application sits at number five on the Alcohol and Tobacco Tax and Trade Bureau's List of Pending American Viticultural Areas Petitions. If approved, the Verde Valley will become Arizona's third AVA after Sonoita and Willcox.

As a supporter of the Arizona wine industry in all its facets, Schumacher was responsible for the formation of the enology program at the Southwest Wine Center at Yavapai College, created to support Arizona's flourishing industry and provide education from viticulture to entrepreneurship through its on-site vineyard, tasting room, science lab and winery.

The vineyard at the Yavapai College Clarkdale campus has grown from the initial plot donated by Keenan to its current fourteen acres of vineyard, which serves as a working lab for its students. The winery and tasting room were built in 2013, and guests who visit the Southwest Wine Center's tasting room are served by current students. Since its first class in 2008, the school has seen graduates—such as Valerie and Daniel Wood of Heart Wood Cellars, Julia Dixon of Defiant Vineyards and Emil Molin of Cove Mesa— go on to start their own wine labels or plant their own vineyards.

At the time that Schumacher became involved, he was the executive dean at Yavapai College. "I was charged by my president to find a unique niche that would make us one-of-a-kind as far as a rural community college," recalls Schumacher. "And my pitch to them was to begin a viticulture and enology program, though it was a hard sell for sure. The college had a building that wasn't really utilizing any kind of potential and it had a lot of land, and those were the two things that we really needed to get things going."

Encouraged by friends in the wine industry to experience the event as part of his program research, Schumacher made a trip to Sacramento to attend the Unified Wine & Grape Symposium. Accompanied by the economic development director from the City of Cottonwood, they agreed that if the wine industry was to get a stronger foothold, it needed an educational component for validity. "With that in mind, I pitched the program to my president, and fortunately, he was visionary enough to accept the challenge. I remember his exact words: 'I want you to move forward with this program. There's one caveat. There's no money.'"

Tom Schumacher judging Yavapai College's Emerging Winemakers Competition. *Tom Schumacher.*

"That was a big challenge," continues Schumacher. "Fortunately, I knew there was somebody that I could at least talk to about it, who had both the vision and the capital to back himself up. And that was Maynard Keenan. We said, here's the deal. We've got a college here. We have a green light on starting the program, but what I need is an actual working vineyard. We went around and around with contracts at the college because some people were still not sold on the idea, but we finally agreed on leasing him an acre of land and he could put in whatever varietal he wanted."

The first classes were offered in the summer of 2008. "It started out with a non-accredited program," Schumacher explains. "They let you run the class three times to see what your enrollment is, and then it gets evaluated by the curriculum committee, who then recommend the program. Well, that first class had over twenty students, which was a really good sign, and then the subsequent classes were full with a waitlist. I enrolled in the classes myself because if I'm going to speak in public, I felt it was a good idea if I really kind of knew what I was talking about," he laughs. "So I'm enrolled in both the viticulture and enology program and I'm still chipping away at it." In 2013, the Southwest Wine Center opened as a sustainable on-campus winery featuring crushing, barreling and bottling facilities and a student-run tasting room.

Initially hired to build the art department (Schumacher had created the Rhode Island School of Design's ceramics program), he has since returned to his roots as an art professor, and his ceramic pieces are displayed in the Southwest Wine Center's tasting room. He also had a hand in the award-winning student-crafted 2017 Amphoria rosé. Part of the curriculum is for students to make their own wine, and Schumacher had a project in mind. "I have a hundred-year-old house in Cottonwood with old pomegranate trees, and I was going to make a pomegranate wine," he recounts. "So I figured I'd make it in a classic Greek-style amphora." After creating a replica of the ancient storage vessel, his plan was thwarted when a heavy frost decimated his pomegranate crop, and Schumacher donated his amphora to Michael Pierce, the director of enology at the college. He, in turn, used it as an aging container for some of his students' wine. The result? The wine, made with Sangiovese grapes grown in the college vineyard and aged in the amphora, won the Grower's Cup at the azcentral Arizona Wine Competition for best rosé that year. With the amphora made from clay sourced from the same vineyard where the grapes were grown, "well, you can't get any closer to the terroir than that," Schumacher says with a laugh.

Southwest Wine Center student wines. *Christian Burns McBeth.*

"I'm very proud of the viticulture and enology program here at the college," says Schumacher, who notes that the Southwest Wine Center has strengthened the industry. "All the graduates that are successful and winning awards for their wines? That's pretty impressive for a relatively new program."

THE SOUTHWEST WINE CENTER

"Tom had a lot of pushback in the beginning," says Michael Pierce, director of enology at Yavapai College, of the early days of the program's formation, as he leads a tour of the Southwest Wine Center. "The college said they didn't really want students making wine—college and alcohol, they don't go together, right? The way Tom sold it to them was to not think of wine as the end product. You know what the end product is? It's developing a culture. Once wine shows up, food shows up, art shows up, tourism shows up. And he was right. Look what happened in Old Town Cottonwood. Now we need more hotels, we need more restaurants."

Among Pierce's additional responsibilities are serving as legislative chair for the Arizona Winegrowers Association and as the winemaker for the two labels owned by his family, Bodega Pierce and the small-batch reserves of Saeculum Cellars. Their Willcox vineyard was Jon Marcus's former Crop Circle Vineyard, renamed Rolling View as a nod to the Pierce family's Rolling View Farm in Nebraska, and supplies the grapes for both labels. His parents, Dan and Barbara, manage the vineyard, and Pierce designs the Saeculum labels and makes the wine in Camp Verde as a tenant of Four Eight Wineworks. On their eighty-acre property in the heart of the Willcox Bench, twenty-seven acres are under vine and eighteen varietals are grown, including Malvasia Bianca, Graciano and Muscat of Alexandria. The plan is to move production to their new tasting room, which opened in 2019 in Clarkdale a quarter mile from Chateau Tumbleweed.

Pierce received a degree in electronic media and visual communication at Northern Arizona University in 2004 and worked in print and web design upon graduating, but while in college, he had taken up brewing and winemaking as a hobby with his father. Advancing their education, they enrolled in the University of California–Davis extension program and then Washington State University. Pierce spent time gaining experience in New Zealand, Australia and Delegat's Wine Estate in Oregon before returning to Arizona. In 2010, he accepted a position as cellar hand at Arizona Stronghold Vineyards, was promoted to assistant winemaker in 2012 and became winemaker in 2013. In 2014, Pierce left to develop his own labels and joined the faculty at the Southwest Wine Center at Yavapai College.

Pierce gestures at the Founders Wall outside the entrance of the $2.5 million Southwest Wine Center. "The college didn't have money for the brand-new program, so they needed to reach out to the community. That wall recognizes all the large gift-givers of $5,000 or more, so the majority of this building was either private donations or grant money." In previous years, wine was made from grapes donated by Maynard Keenan and sourced from Willcox, but 2018 was the first year that wine was sourced completely from the campus vineyard. "We had twenty-five tons come off," says Pierce proudly. "We were actually even able to sell to some graduates in the program."

Pierce opens the door to a compact lab. "This lab equipment was paid with a grant by the National Science Foundation," he explains. "This is one lab set-up, and in the chemistry department we have ten of these. We can test alcohol, pH, TA, free and total SO2, malic—all done right here. My students really don't know how lucky they are. When I was taking my courses, I had to read about all that; I didn't get to do it." In the humidity-

Michael Pierce with Valerie and Daniel Wood of Heart Wood Cellars. *Christian Burns McBeth.*

controlled barrel room, Pierce rests his hand on the amphora made by Tom Schumacher for that winning rosé. "This produced twenty-seven gallons, about half a barrel. You get a big award and you have half a barrel's worth," says Pierce with a rueful smile.

Next to gleaming stainless-steel vats in the tank room sits a sand-colored concrete ovoid. Hearkening back to the ancient method of fermenting wine in concrete tanks, this revived trend has found a home at the Southwest Wine Center. Made by a company called Sonoma Cast Stone, the concrete egg weighs 4,500 pounds. "Normal concrete has a lot of lime, which would affect the acid profile, so the composition is made appropriate for wine," explains Pierce as he tells the story of its procurement. "I had called them just to get a price. I knew we wanted something, but they're cost-prohibitive at about $15,000 apiece. Well, he said, let me get back to you, and he called back and said, 'I've got an egg that you can have.' It went to Gallo as a demo model, but it was the wrong color, and Gallo sent it back, so it was sitting in their warehouse. Apparently, they talked to Todd at Dos Cabezas, because he had ordered one, and asked, 'Is this program for real? Because I'm about to give one away.' So that worked out," he says with a grin.

One of the goals of the Southwest Wine Center is to create a data collection and information-sharing repository delineating various growing conditions. "For example," says Pierce, "here at the college we have one block that's super clay-rich and the rootstocks are not doing very good, but the same rootstock in our rocky block is doing excellent. So we have to manage water because the clay really binds the water, and it becomes almost anaerobic. And then it also affects nutrient uptake, so we're having to amend the soil to make sure the nutrients are available to the vine." Pierce points to a display of soils in the Southwest Wine Center tasting room. "If you look at them closely, you'll notice one is super clumped up—that's the clay that I'm talking about—and the other is rocky and sandy and loose. And they're both from our little site here. Hopefully the students take away this information so that when they look at a site, even though the realtor might say 'vineyard potential' on their listing, they need to quite literally put the shovel in the earth. They need to feel soil, check the slope, the sun exposure, what's the water; do you have all the things that you need?"

Accommodations in the curriculum are made for the students, many of whom hold down full-time jobs while attending their classes. "A lot of them come from Phoenix," notes Pierce, "and the program is scheduled to be supportive of that with evening classes and weekend labs." The school also prepares the students for the financial expectations of starting a new venture. "Many graduates of this program are successful people," notes Pierce. "They have a little bit of money, but they need to use it wisely and learn how to get the best return from that investment and not spend it up front since it will be years before you get your dollars back. If you're going to grow a vineyard, it's going to be four years before you have any grapes, and then if you're going to make the wine, it's going to be another two years before you're in the market. So maybe you should start with the wine, source some fruit and get your brand going as your vineyard starts up."

Exploring those grape varietals that do best in Arizona's unique climate is also part of the curriculum. "Graciano is probably my favorite," says Pierce. "I love it. It has great structure but also good acid. We've got a lot of Petite Sirah, which people really like, but in our warm climate the acidity isn't retained, whereas Graciano has good pH, good acid and that same concentration, but people don't know it. We're also working with more experimental things here. We have what we call the BRA block, which is our Barbera, Refosco and Aglianico. I think of those three, the Aglianico has the highest potential to be award-winning. It's got a lot of structure to it. It's not something you're going to barrel age for six months. It's going to be eighteen months, and it's going to be an intense, serious wine, not a wimpy wine. I think consumers will respond if we're patient with it and give it time. I'm really looking forward to the days when we can get some sort of defined character from this region," continues Pierce. "Wines from Sonoita are different than wines from Willcox. I don't think there's enough mass of wines from the Verde Valley to get that character yet, but we're getting there."

"My students are the lucky ones," says Pierce. "My dad and I wanted to go to a school like this ten years ago, but nothing existed, so we had to leave the state. We ended up at Washington State, where I was very happy with the education, but it didn't provide this. I mean, we didn't have fourteen acres to work with and a full winery. Even though it's five years in, we have a wine club that's full, we have a vineyard that's producing fruit and we're starting to understand the challenges within each block. Last year, we sold about 600 cases. This harvest, we've produced 1,200 cases, and we have eighty people on our waitlist for the wine club. And we actually were able to win a couple pretty great awards. I think great things are still to come."

Jim Cunningham, general manager at Maynard Keenan's Merkin Vineyards Scottsdale, is one of the successful graduates who helped the Southwest Wine Center win an award. In 2016, he was working in the restaurant wine industry and deciding on his next step. Many of his peers were taking the sommelier route, but for Cunningham, "I wanted to get a little closer and kind of get my hands dirty. I just happened to stumble across the article about the wine program, and I thought, yes, this is exactly what I want to do. Learn how to actually make it instead of just teach people about it." He especially appreciated the comprehensive program and his passionate classmates. "I loved being immersed in the wine culture that's developing here in Arizona," he says. "Everybody that was in the program really wanted to be there. They made sacrifices to attend classes to be part of the program and had built a strong community. A lot of those people that I went to class with are now working with vineyards and with wineries, and they're developing their own place here in Arizona."

A highlight of the program was his role in one of the college's award-winning wines. As part of the curriculum, all the students have a hand in making wine at the Southwest Wine Center. "We would have blending trials with things we were starting to ferment. We would taste them, come up with some of our own blends, submit that and the top ideas went to

Wine grapes at Alcantara Vineyards. *Author's collection.*

a vote. And one of the blends that I selected was one of the top wines, so we barreled and bottled it. And it actually was one of the winners of the azcentral Wine Competition," he says proudly. "My name is on the label and I wrote the label notes. It was my blend, but I can't take all the credit, of course. Everyone in the program at that time had their hands on it, and it was a lot of fun."

Upon graduating in 2018, Cunningham worked as a food and beverage director for a small hotel brand for a time but missed a greater connection to Arizona wine. He feels that with his position at the Merkin Vineyards tasting room, he has found his niche. "I was doing a lot more administrative and hotel work and felt I was getting too far from Arizona wine. I wanted to get back, and I didn't know how I was going to do that. And then this came up and it was just perfect."

"Yavapai College and the Southwest Wine Center program ends up generating a new workforce," acknowledges Keenan. "There are people who want to be a vineyard guy, who want to be a winemaker, work at a winery or own their own winery. And then there are others who get in and realize, this isn't for me, but now they enter the service industry in a restaurant or a bottle shop or hotel management with a better understanding of what the industry is."

THE ARIZONA VIGNERONS ALLIANCE

In March 2016, the Arizona Vignerons Alliance launched with the clear and ambitious objective to define a labeling qualification standard for wines that are 100 percent grown and produced in Arizona. Founded by Kelly and Todd Bostock of Dos Cabezas WineWorks, Kent and Lisa Callaghan of Callaghan Vineyards, Maynard and Jennifer Keenan of Caduceus Cellars and Rob and Sarah Hammelman of Sand-Reckoner Vineyards, their mission, as outlined on their AVA website, "is to ensure quality and authenticity in Arizona wine; to improve grape growing and winemaking across all wine regions of the state; to help promote Arizona wines so they are recognized, respected and sought-after in Arizona, the U.S., and globally."

The founding board was inspired by groups such as France's Club Trésors in Champagne and Italy's Denominazione di Origine Controllata e Garantita (DOCG), which were formed to set standards and identify the correlation between quality wine and provenance. All wines submitted for Arizona Vignerons Alliance certification must be produced in the state, made from 100 percent Arizona-grown fruit and include comprehensive data of soil types, elevation and growing conditions and chemistry analyses such as pH and brix. The Arizona Vignerons Alliance's aim is to collect and share this valuable information to aid fellow winemakers and growers in identifying the regions and varietals best suited to advance quality standards.

At the AVA launch event, supporters such as Kimber Lanning, founder of Local First Arizona; Julie Murphree of the Arizona Farm Bureau; and Michael Pierce took to the stage to voice their confidence in the newly formed group. "It's very exciting," said Pierce at the time. "I think they have the foresight and resolution to start this new project, and we really want to show our support as a college and educational institution."

Two months later, on May 9, 2016, the first certification panel was held at Vinum 55 at Scottsdale Hangar One. The blind tasting was moderated by Dale Sparks, wine importer and founder of Quench Wines and 220 Imports. As the judging panel of twelve experienced sommeliers and industry professionals was sequestered in a downstairs room, eighty-six wines were poured into numbered decanters and presented to the judges, and sixty-four became the first Arizona Vignerons Alliance certified wines.

Now in its third year, the AVA is also working toward its mission statement to establish awareness of the world-class wines being made in Arizona. The annual Arizona Vignerons Alliance Symposium at the

Arizona Vignerons Alliance event. *Christian Burns McBeth.*

Farm at South Mountain has become Phoenix's premier Arizona wine education event, offering attendees an itinerary of morning seminars, a midday wine-paired meal and an afternoon grand tasting of AVA-certified wines to meet the winemakers. The informative seminars also serve to introduce acclaimed international wine professionals to the industry in the Grand Canyon State. Esteemed guests such as Swiss grape geneticist and author Dr. José Vouillamoz, author and wine critic Patrick Comiskey of the *Los Angeles Times*, writer Elaine Chukan Brown of Hawk Wakawaka Wine Reviews and master sommelier and master of wine Doug Frost have all sat on past panels.

Though the AVA has been met with some controversy from fellow winemakers concerned about it being divisive, Kelly Bostock is quick to point out that the intent is to benefit all. "We wanted to create an industry-specific organization to make Arizona wine better by collecting data to pinpoint what makes certain sites unique in producing good wines," she explains. "There are so many pieces to it that are valuable, not just for up-and-coming wineries, but established wineries too. It's become such a positive force, and we're excited about it. It makes perfect sense. In wine-growing regions, when you see those types of labels on the bottle, you know it's tried and tested. There's that element, but also education and marketing. We're bringing in wine writers, and we have a team of lobbyists helping serve our best interests when it comes to wine laws. All in all, I think there's a spot for it in Arizona history."

Maynard Keenan agrees. "We need to get together and share notes," he emphasizes. "I think some of the criticism was that we think we know what we're doing and we're being elitist. No," Keenan says emphatically, "what we're saying is we don't know what we're doing. We're trying to figure it out. We're willing to admit that we're wrong in a lot of things, we need to ask the right questions and we need to talk about it and gather the information to taste perfection in the glass and raise the bar."

EXPERIMENTATION AND DEFINING VARIETALS

Because Arizona is still finding its way, it's in the unique position for its pioneering winegrowers to experiment with lesser-known varietals that thrive in its high-elevation climates. "We don't have some sort of consumer demand that says, okay, Arizona wine is this," says Michael Pierce. "We haven't really defined ourselves, which is exciting because you're not pigeonholed." At Rolling View Vineyard, his father is growing an ancient vine called Muscat of Alexandria, part of the parentage of Malvasia Bianca, a grape that is fast rising as one of the signatures of Arizona's terroir. "It's an ancient variety that has not been hybridized and has unique characteristics to it that haven't been bred out—real spindly, loose clusters with big grapes that are almost the size of table grapes. It's really tough to press and we don't get a good yield, but the resulting wines are awesome, and we're going to plant more. We make it in a dry, acid-forward, food-friendly style, which people don't expect from a Muscat. I worked a harvest in 2009 in Oregon, and we made a heck of a lot of Pinot, a little bit of Pinot Gris and a little bit of Chardonnay, and that's their list," he continues. "That's just what their climate allows them to do. They couldn't grow the eighteen varieties that we do in our vineyard."

In 2019, famed grape geneticist Dr. José Vouillamoz traveled from Switzerland to speak at the Symposium of the Arizona Vignerons Alliance and shared his fascinating views on Arizona and its similarities to unique wine-growing areas of the world. In collaboration with local growers, he compiled an astonishing list of "at least" forty-five varietals currently being cultivated in Arizona. "It's a huge diversity for such a small wine region."

In his presentation, he shared that Arizona's climate might favor narrowing down the selection to Mediterranean varietals grown in such regions as Spain, southern Italy, southern France, Greece and Turkey. "I was thinking as a European about American wines," he said. "When we think Oregon, we say Pinot Noir; when we think Finger Lakes, we say Riesling; when we think California, we say Bordeaux blends. When we think Arizona—sorry, we don't know that you grow wine here," he said to laughter from the crowd. "Maybe your solution would be Malvasia or Garnacha." Pointing to a map, Vouillamoz suggested focusing on those grapes that are grown in the Mediterranean regions he had outlined—Graciano, Barbera, Sangiovese, Vermentino, Aglianico, Tannat. He also proposed five varietals "that I love very much that are not planted yet outside their region of origin," such as Verdejo from Spain, Nerello Mascalese from Sicily, Assyrtiko from Greece, Emir from Turkey and Areni from Armenia.

Maple & Ash wine director Jason Cabellero agrees. "I feel like we're going to be able to get behind a centralized identity of a grape. Right now we're narrowing it down to a few, but we're going to find that hero grape or group of grapes that really does well in this climate that people will have a lot of success with. I think we're turning that corner."

Kief-Joshua Vineyards in Elgin. *Becky Limberg.*

Jason Caballero and Mark Tarbell. *Author's collection.*

"José Vouillamoz basically confirmed what we've thought all along," says Maynard Keenan, "that there's a Mediterranean strata that makes sense here. With the Rhone varieties, Grenache and Mourvedre do well here, but that's because they're actually Garnacha and Monastrell from Spain. Tempranillo does well here. Malvasia Bianca di Piemonte does well here. So if we look at that strata, now you're looking at Barbera, Graciano, Tempranillo, Sangiovese, Sagrantino; all those things fall into that belt. Areni from Armenia might be perfect here. Nerello Mascalese might work because of the elevation and latitude. José's looking at the math, and I'm the artist looking at the expression in the cellar, but you need to have your feet on the ground first."

Cody Chase Burkett can be found in the tasting room of Autumn Sage Vineyards in Sonoita and is the founder of AZ Wine Monk ("monk" because Burkett had once attended seminary to become a Greek Orthodox priest). He has become the state's most prolific Arizona wine reviewer via his website and podcast and has coined the term "winarchy." "We're more willing to throw caution to the wind, so to speak, and try new things," he says. "We're willing to buck against the trend. When Arizona wine first started out, it tried to be like everywhere else. Let's plant Chardonnay, let's plant Pinot Noir. And then we were willing to say, these things don't work, let's try some weird stuff. Cab Sauv doesn't work, but what about Petit Verdot? Okay, that works great. Chardonnay works some years, some years it doesn't. Okay, let's try Malvasia Bianca, which is a brilliant choice. I remember Michael Pierce telling me that when they first got Rolling View, it had been fallow from Jon Marcus for years, and the only vines that were producing and thriving, even with neglect, were the Malvasia vines. So that's a grape that wants to be here. And I've been talking about Emir for five years since I came back from Turkey! I honestly think that we'll see varietals from Turkey, from Palestine, from Lebanon, from Greece. These are going to be varietals that'll be part of the future of Arizona winemaking. Emil Molin already has Assyrtiko planted in his Cove Mesa Vineyard in Cornville."

Burkett predicts that the future of winemaking includes the exploration of new regions of Arizona for grape-growing. "I think we're going to start seeing an expansion," says Burkett. "Gila County right now has a lot of potential area near Young and Globe. You have Bruzzi Vineyard in Young growing vines that are essentially above the Mogollon Rim at seven thousand feet. He's growing Vidal Blanc, a varietal that you

Cody Burkett, the AZ Wine Monk, at Cabal Cellars. *Author's collection.*

would associate with ice wines in Canada. And I predict Chino Valley and Paulden will come on line as Arizona's fourth AVA in the next fifteen years. It's the only place in Arizona where you can grow Pinot Noir consistently well. The soils there are a little bit more volcanic, while most of the other vineyards in Arizona have an alluvial nature. Del Rio Springs Vineyard in Paulden—Rick and Maricor Skladzien are wonderful people—already have a couple vintages of Pinot under their belt, and they also grow fun hybrid varietals like Vignoles that aren't being grown anywhere else in the state."

Chef James Porter is planning one of the newest vineyards, which will be established in the Prescott National Forest. Porter and his wife, Wendy, will soon open Terra Farm + Manor, a culinary lodge on an eighty-five-acre property offering a farm for harvesting on-site, a cooking school with nationally acclaimed visiting chefs and a vineyard to produce wine exclusively for the guests. A longtime supporter of local sourcing, Porter hosted locavore dinners at his acclaimed Scottsdale restaurant Tapino, where guests would dine with farmers and Arizona winemakers. Porter's fifty-wines-by-the-glass list included flights of Arizona wine, and he shares stories of a humorous initial meeting with Sam Pillsbury, whose label was the first he added to his menu, and drinking wine with Maynard Keenan until the wee hours on the restaurant patio. At Terra Farm + Manor, he'll be partnering up with two friends, winemaker Adam LaZarre of LaZarre Wines and Jason Yeager, vineyard manager for Niner Wine Estates, to plant a four-and-a-half-acre plot. Drawn to the ancient vineyards of Bekaa Valley in Lebanon and wineries such as Chateau Musar, he's inspired by that history. "I'm not getting into the wine business to sell wine. I'm getting into the wine business because I want to learn how to do it," says Porter. "Let's do it how they did it at Chateau Musar. Look at the technology two hundred years ago. That's the technology I want to use. Unless we need a tractor," he laughs. "Other than that, you know, let's figure it out. If they were able to make it, we can make it."

Changes Needed in the Industry

To continue to make strides, bureaucratic hurdles must be overcome and outdated laws addressed. Incorporated in 1983, the Arizona Wine Growers Association was formed to further the upward trajectory of Arizona's wine industry and to effect changes in the laws that stifle its growth. As a past three-term president of the Arizona Wine Growers Association, Rod Keeling has had a hand in working on legislative decisions affecting Arizona's winemakers, including the bill that would have taken away the winemakers' right to self-distribute in the wake of the 2005 U.S. Supreme Court Granholm decision. "I worked on the Granholm decision where the distributors basically tried to strip us of all our farm winery rights, but we were able to come to a compromise of some sort," he explains. "The capacity limit on our production has always been there, but it used to be seventy-five thousand gallons. They brought it down to twenty thousand if you wanted to self-distribute, and that law passed in 2006." He notes, however, that even with the new restrictions, it had a positive effect in spurring the interest in Arizona as a wine-growing region. "You know, there were only nine licensed wineries in Arizona in 2005," says Keeling. "We were number nine. After we passed that bill, we got so much visibility in the media, and we also got certainty in the law, and I think those two things contributed to our growth and attracted investment in the business. A good law is a great thing, though, now when we look back, we could say we shouldn't have compromised to such a small capacity limit, but we're working on that. We'll get there eventually."

As the current legislative chair for the Arizona Wine Growers Association, Michael Pierce agrees that there is work to be done. "The boom that started in 2006 with licensing allowing for self-distribution opened up the market," he says. "Now we're kind of at a precipice where there's over a hundred winery licenses and there's a few bumping up against the production cap. At twenty thousand gallons, you lose your right to self-distribute, but if we're going to have a good next ten years, we need to get that cap raised so wineries can grow. Twenty thousand gallons is not very much; it's 8,300 cases."

John McLoughlin of Cellar 433 believes the state can do much more to help support the industry. "They could help us with grants where I don't have to hire a professional for $5,000 or $6,000 to write it. Years ago, I wrote one grant and I was beaten by the State of Arizona...for a grant that was being given by the State of Arizona," he says with some exasperation. There is also the frustration in obtaining vineyard loans. "The state could really help us with public awareness and low-interest and vineyard loans. I can walk into any Wells Fargo in California and say I'd like a loan for a vineyard. 'Sure. Just a second. Let me get our loan specialist who deals with vineyards.' Here you say you'd like to talk to a vineyard loan specialist, and they say, 'You do what? We don't do that in Arizona.'"

Community Support

"I'm an Arizona native, but I've seen more of the state chasing wine than I had ever before." For Richard Ruelas, a reporter for the *Arizona Republic*, a serendipitous discovery in the Verde Valley led to his Arizona wine passion. "We were headed to Oak Creek Brewery, made a wrong turn and ended up driving by Page Springs," he recalls. "We saw a sign that said wine tasting and popped in. And that was it." He and his wife, Georgann Yara, a fellow journalist, stopped at all the area's wineries, including Caduceus, and his first wine story in 2009 featured Maynard Keenan. "After that first story on Caduceus, I just found more great stories," he says as he shares a humorous tale about pushing Dick Erath's car out of a ditch in Willcox. "The readers kept reading them, and so it's been a bit of a mini-beat ever since." Ruelas was also instrumental in organizing the state's most prestigious competition, the azcentral Arizona Wine Competition. In 2010, Todd Bostock, as a board member of the Arizona Wine Growers Association, approached Ruelas about having the newspaper handle the logistics of the new wine competition as an independent organizer "so that they wouldn't be essentially giving awards to themselves," explains Ruelas. "I thought, sure, how hard can this be?" he laughs. "That was when there were just a few dozen entries. Now it's grown to over 250 entries and takes up much of my November and December." He is proud of the exposure it brings to the industry. "People take our lists of the state's best wines with them to the wine festivals, and winemakers tell us they see them with the tasting room guides we print. I think our readers get excited about traveling in Arizona, trying unique wine and experiencing something different. A lot of Phoenix restaurants and wine shops are increasingly carrying Arizona wine and celebrating it, partially fueled, I would like to hope, by our coverage."

Barb Coons, owner of Four Tails Vineyard, is grateful for the community support. As current president of the Arizona Wine Growers Association, she would also like to see more members get involved and for the community to rally around its winemakers. Educating consumers and getting more Arizona wine poured in local restaurants is something the AWGA is working on. "Some of the goals from a strategic priority perspective is engaging more members and more winemakers to be a part of the association and really pitch in to tell our story," she says. "If you look at the landscape across Arizona, it's a bunch of hardworking farmers and winemakers making some really great wine, and exposure within restaurants will really help elevate that," says Coons. "We need that exposure and for restaurants to consistently carry Arizona wine. Not walking into a restaurant, asking for it and have someone say, 'Arizona makes wine?'"

Across the state, Arizona wines are making a slow but steady incremental appearance on restaurant menus and in wine bars and bottle shops. At Hidden Track Bottle Shop in downtown Phoenix, Danielle Middlebrook and Craig Dziadowicz not only shine a spotlight on Arizona wines with their large selection but are also collaborating with Michael Pierce on a special series of their own. In 2018, a trio of Arizona-centric wine bars opened to supplement vineyard tasting rooms. GenuWine in Phoenix features a self-serve Wine Emotion dispensing system with an extensive local wine list inspired by owners Emily Rieve's and Lindsey Schoenemann's trips to Arizona wine country. In Jerome, Ginger Mackenzie's inviting Vino Zona offers Arizona wine, mead and cider in a cozy setting that feels like your quirky aunt's parlor. Stop in Tucson at the Arizona Wine Collective, boasting one of the state's largest selections of Arizona wine (plus local brews and Arizona kombucha), and you'll find patrons enjoying flights at the bar or sharing a bottle on the fountain-side patio.

Waverly Brown pours her family's Callaghan wine at the AZ Wine Collective tasting room in Tucson. *Author's collection.*

At Joel Latondress and Lara Mulchay's Arcadia Premium market, Latondress shares his extensive knowledge to help customers select a bottle from the twenty Arizona wines they carry. "In a retail market still dominated by Chardonnay, Pinot Noir and Cabernet Sauvignon," says Latondress, "I love that Arizona producers are able to find their voice in Rhone varietals such as Grenache, Syrah and Mourvedre made in a style that often pairs well with food and shows off the terroir. It's exciting to see the innovation in Arizona winemaking and how the winemakers of today are shaping our future as a place of distinction among emerging wine regions in the United States."

Well known for her spectacular desserts, pastry chef Tracy Dempsey opened ODV Wine with her husband, Chuck, in Tempe in 2017 to feature small-lot, boutique wineries, including a heavy emphasis on Arizona winemakers. "We still have people come in who make a face when you mention Arizona wine, but we view it as an opportunity to educate and give them a taste," Dempsey says. "But then we'll have somebody like the woman a couple of weeks ago asking for Deep Sky. She's returned twice, so she's obviously an Arizona wine fan." Dempsey is also finding her twice-monthly Arizona meet-your-winemaker events and classes very popular. Most recently, Sam Pillsbury and Kent Callaghan spent an evening answering questions, and Cody Burkett held a Rosé All Day wine class. "The Arizona Vignerons Alliance is a big supporter of ours," says Dempsey, "and I love introducing people to what the winemakers are doing."

In Agritopia, a visionary urban farm community in Gilbert, founder Joe Johnston has built a craftsmen village of local artisans featuring shops, micro-restaurants and a brewery, along with a home for Arizona vinifera at a winery and wine bar called Garage-East. "This will be a partnership between a local family that lives in Agritopia and Todd Bostock from Dos Cabezas to push the limits in the pioneering spirit of what is wine," Johnston described on a 2016 hard-hat tour. "For the groundbreaking, they made a wine using Roussanne grapes from Sonoita, apples, and mesquite honey and it was delicious!" A collaborative venture between the Bostocks and Brian and Megan Ruffentine, Garage-East experiments with fermentation methods and creative grape and fruit blends. The grape crushing and production takes place in Sonoita, while the Ruffentines are in charge of day-to-day operations and clever iterations such as their playful Breakfast Wine, made with grapes and juice from fruit harvested at the farm, and the popular Sonoran Spritz, a bottled sparkling cocktail made with white wine, local citrus and herbs. Wines from Dos Cabezas

WineWorks and other Arizona labels are also poured, such as Oddity, Chateau Tumbleweed, Caduceus, Callaghan and Rune. "Another fun thing about it," says partner Kelly Bostock, "is we're moving to a green winery. We're using almost 100 percent kegs, and right now we're up to eight tap handles."

Executive chef Jeremy Pacheco of the historic Hermosa Inn is a longtime proponent of supporting local purveyors, and that includes wine growers. Visit this award-winning luxury boutique property in Paradise Valley, and you'll find a wine list with a rotating selection of approximately twenty-five Arizona wines. He remembers being introduced to Pillsbury Wine Company's Viognier at a Dine Out with the Chefs event at Scottsdale Center. "That's when I really started to appreciate Arizona wines," Pacheco recalls. Keeling-Schaefer and Dos Cabezas were early wine selections on the menu, and 2010 marked the inaugural Arizona wine dinner held at Lon's at the Hermosa Inn featuring winemaker Corey Turnbull of Burning Tree Cellars and the wines of Arizona Stronghold, Page Spring Cellars, Burning Tree Cellars, Cellar Dweller and Caduceus. That and subsequent dinners proved to be so popular that the Hermosa Inn now hosts annual Spring and Fall Harvest dinners designed around local purveyors and guest winemakers. "We just had a wine dinner with Eric Glomski. I sent him the menu, he paired wines and we spent a Friday afternoon tasting his wines. I'll tell you, we tasted twelve; there wasn't a bad one in the bunch, and that speaks volumes. His brandy is pretty awesome too."

"One of the things that makes me happy about hosting these wine dinners," continues Pacheco, "is being able to show people who haven't tried Arizona wines what Arizona is capable of doing. It's exciting to see the industry evolving, to see the awards this year for Pillsbury, Callaghan, Dos Cabezas and all the other wineries that are really starting to get noticed. For me, the wine industry is a huge part of supporting Arizona agriculture. For them to see success means success for all of Arizona."

Sommelier Kevin Lewis—wine director at Kai at the Sheraton Grand at Wild Horse Pass in Chandler, Arizona's only five-star, five-diamond restaurant—concurs and continues to host a series of dinners dedicated to Arizona wineries. Lewis recalls his earliest exposure was a trip to Sonoita around 2008. "Our somm Erik Johnson—he's now the head sommelier at the French Laundry—had put together a trip for the restaurant team to go to Callaghan Vineyard, work in the vineyard and graft vines." Another local winery he recalls making an impression was Sand-Reckoner Vineyards.

Kevin Lewis, wine director at Kai at the Sheraton Grand at Wild Horse Pass. *Debby Wolvos Photography.*

"The somm before me, Thomas Klafke, had brought in a few of their wines, including a Syrah that was just great. When I took over the position, I wanted to see what else was out there and stumbled across Rune on Instagram and sent a DM to James. He came up the next week, I tasted through his lineup and brought in his Wild Syrah by the glass. From that, it just kind of blossomed into a constant search and exploration to taste what people are doing. The guys on the staff really dig the Sand-Reckoner Malvasia, the Dos Cabezas rosé is a great food wine in terms of pairing and I'm a huge fan of Chateau Tumbleweed."

"When people look at a wine list, they'll be hesitant to spend upwards of eighty or ninety dollars on a bottle of Arizona wine," Lewis notes, "but they'll readily spend that and more on a California wine because they're familiar with it. Part of the reason I wanted to offer the Rune Wild Syrah by the glass was to make it more affordable and to entice people to step outside of their comfort zone and try something different, something from Arizona. And when I can fit an Arizona wine into a tasting menu, I definitely love to do that. One, because, well, you're kind of stuck with me and what pairings I pour," he laughs, "but also it's getting that exposure out there to people who otherwise wouldn't venture out of the more popular regions."

Like the Arizona wines he supports, chef and restaurateur Mark Tarbell has won his fair share of acclaim and accolades, both for his restaurant Tarbell's and Tarbell's Tavern and for his cooking prowess. He is a 2007 *Iron Chef America* winner, two-time inductee into the Arizona Culinary Hall of Fame, James Beard award nominee and recipient of numerous local awards and recognition. He's cooked for some of the world's culinary icons, including Julia Child, and is just as comfortable entertaining celebrity friends as he is chatting with local chefs as host of his PBS TV show *Plate and Pour*. Wine, however, remains as big a love as food. He is a wine columnist for the *Arizona Republic* newspaper and since 1989 has sat on the judging panel for the prestigious Los Angeles International Wine Competition, one of the oldest and largest wine judging competitions in the world. "I'm one of the longest-running judges, and it's very interesting," says Tarbell. "The judges have always been a group of master sommeliers, masters of wines and winemakers from all over the world. Usually it's about eighty of us, and we judge somewhere between three thousand and four thousand wines over three days."

Tarbell was one of the earliest culinary pros to tip his hat to Arizona's winemakers, including scoring Sam Pillsbury's first vintage, the Roan Red, a ninety-three in his newspaper review, helping to propel the new winery into public awareness. An Arizona resident since 1986, Tarbell's early exposure was to "the kitschy touristy wines," but he didn't let that deter him. "I am a very curious person by nature, and Mr. Callaghan in Sonoita has been the real deal since day one. He is really an amazing winemaker; I can't say enough good about him. There are lots of characters in our wine business here in Arizona, and all contribute something very important. You have Todd Bostock and his wife at Dos Cabezas, just wonderful people who are making really great wine. You have characters like Sam Pillsbury and people like Sand-Reckoner, and then Pavle, one of the biggest supporters. He's not only a great guy, but he's also very smart and was one of the earliest supporters in a big way that was meaningful.

"Maynard really is a beacon," he continues. "You can't deny the power of people paying attention because of who he is and his career in music, but he really has a tremendous amount of passion and integrity and a lot of knowledge. He's a very, very knowledgeable food and wine person and very passionate about it. And combining all those things with the fact that he can create a lot of buzz and attention, well, that really helps Arizona as a whole. The national spotlight comes on us a lot more readily because of

Mark Tarbell (*center foreground*) with the winemakers of Callaghan, Dos Cabezas, Sand-Reckoner, Chateau Tumbleweed and Pillsbury at Tarbell's restaurant. *Christian Burns McBeth.*

a guy like him. And then when you add that he really cares about making the best he can, I'm grateful for him, and I imagine most people in Arizona are to a degree.

"People I know in the wine business outside of Arizona are watching it very closely and even making inquiries as to how to make an investment, and that's good because the inquiries show that Arizona is on the map. There are so many characters in the business that are all trying to survive and do the best they can and do something for Arizona in their own way," says Tarbell. "There are a number of really integrous winemakers that are doing things in a wonderful way because they're picking varietals that are unusual. My vision, my hope for Arizona, is that people at some point generationally will get bored with Pinot, Chard and Cab, and they'll be looking for something else."

Sommelier T. Scott Stephens, co-owner of Beckett's Table and Southern Rail in Phoenix, worked at Tarbell's and credits Tarbell for instilling in him a passion for wine and commitment to service and hospitality. He also played an important role in Stephens meeting his wife, as they both were part of the opening crew, Scott as a bartender and Katie as a server. Now twenty-five years later, the sommelier couple are partners with Justin and Michelle Beckett in the two successful restaurants they manage, with Katie serving as wine director for Beckett's Table and Scott at Southern Rail.

"It's interesting to me when you have moments of epiphany that alter the course of your thought process, and that's what happened over at Beckett's." Stephens is speaking of his first taste of a wine made at the hands of one of Arizona's gifted winemakers. "Katie and I were diving deep into Barolo, Barbaresco, French wine and everything else in between, but we never looked in our own backyard," he admits. Having sold his company where he built luxury wine cellars for multimillion-dollar properties, the next chapter of his career was decided when he agreed to partner with Beckett to open Beckett's Table in 2010. "Katie and I set out to have a wine program that would demystify wine and be very approachable with a lot of variety," he explains, "so we had fifty wines by the glass."

Beckett's Table opened to instant success, and Stephens recalls an eventful visit in the spring of 2011. "It's around 2:30 and we're in the middle of it. We've had great reviews, critics love us and we're doing amazing numbers and covers. We're polishing glassware, wiping tables, leveling things, and this couple walks in out of the blue. They don't look like they're older than twenty-five, and they have a couple of bottles of wine in their hands. 'Hi, how are you, we make wine.' I was helping behind the bar and all hell's breaking loose, but on a typical whim, I thought, you know what, a glass of wine sounds really good right now."

Rob and Sarah Hammelman poured a glass of their inaugural vintage of Sand-Reckoner Malvasia, and "I remember it like it was yesterday," says Stephens. "I put my nose to this Malvasia, and wow, I had never smelled so much floral activity, white flowers, blossoms; it was just ridiculous. And then I tasted it, and it had an amazing racy acidity and this mouthfeel. And I asked Rob, I kid you not, three times I asked him, are you sure these are Arizona grapes? 'Yes. They're on my property.' Where is this? 'Willcox.' 'Where the hell is Willcox? And you made this?' 'Yes, I made this.' Then I tried the rosé and was blown away again. It had this huge mouthfeel and structure with great acid just like the Malvasia. I looked like a befuddled yahoo because I'm working off my experience with Arizona's novelty wines. So I pulled Katie over and asked her to try. Katie says, 'Where are these from?' 'Willcox.' 'Where is that?' and the whole conversation repeats itself," Stephens says with a laugh. "At that moment, I looked at Katie, and in front of Rob and Sarah, I said, 'We need to relook at this wine list and go in a direction that highlights Arizona wines.' That afternoon created a kindred relationship between the four of us, and I just love those two to death. That moment changed everything about how Katie and I had been navigating through the wine

Dos Cabezas Águileón. *Kevin Lewis.*

industry, and in the process, we have forged some of the most wonderful friendships that are going to be ours for a lifetime."

"That's how it all began," continues Stephens, "and immediately we bought a case of each." Now you'll find fifteen to twenty Arizona wines at Beckett's Table at any given time and an even larger selection at Southern Rail, their second restaurant, which opened in 2014. "I said, let's really sink our teeth into it; let's make a third of it Arizona," says Stephens, "so we have anywhere from thirty or thirty-five wines from Arizona that rotate, and they're half off on Sundays and Mondays. I've had Greg's Laramita Viognier by the glass for about a year now, Ann Roncone's Montepulciano from Lightning Ridge is a beautiful, elegant wine and Mark at Golden Rule is doing remarkable work. They have a 2016 Syrah that is just super. I mean, it is a crowd-pleaser beyond words. We just put on Bruzzi Vineyards from Young. He has a great Vidal Blanc that's delicious. It's so well made, it's balanced, great acidity, the whole bit. And Katie has Heart Wood's Syrah at Beckett's, which is pretty remarkable too."

Stephens has seen people become more receptive to Arizona wine since Beckett's Table opened ten years ago. Customers are learning that Arizona's winemakers are creating a world-class product, and he's thrilled to introduce new fans. "There's a lot of wine lovers out there. There are people who love supporting local, and they love what we're doing. And we're seeing it. I'm now buying cases at a time on a regular basis at both restaurants every few weeks, if not every week. I'm thrilled to be a part of it, and I can't believe I am."

Wine Festivals Celebrate Arizona

Rhonni and Josh Moffitt were the founders of *Arizona Vines & Wines* magazine (now *AZ Wine Lifestyle*) and experienced firsthand the exciting growth in the last fifteen years. Josh, who works in real estate, saw the value in vineyard land with his first Willcox purchase in 2005 at $2,500 an acre. The couple grew the publication from an 8-page real estate brochure to a 116-page Arizona wine, food and travel resource before selling it in 2013. Over the years, Josh has sold vineyards such as Sweet Sunrise, Bonita Springs and Crop Circle and properties to wineries including Carlson Creek, Zarpara and Aridus.

Rhonni recalls the early days of the publication when she served as executive director for the Arizona Wine Growers Association and on the board of the Verde Valley Wine Consortium. "It was an exciting time, and I thrived on helping a fledgling industry and getting to know the amazing people who were a part of it," she says. "I'm very proud of what we accomplished during the years we published the magazine. The feedback I've received from the winemakers is that it really helped wine lovers throughout the state learn more about the industry, helped increase traffic at the tasting rooms and brought light to the fact that award-winning wine is being made here in the Sunshine State. When we started the magazine in 2008," she remembers, "you could ask twenty Arizona residents if they knew that wine was being made here in Arizona, and you'd be lucky if anyone had any idea. Now, I'm happy to say that it's much more well known. Many dining establishments, wine bars and grocery stores carry local labels, and you can find Arizona wine-based events and festivals on calendars throughout the year, making access to the product so much easier."

Back in 1984, Bill Letarte partnered with the Arizona Wine Growers Association to organize Arizona's first wine festival in Sonoita. As Erik Berg documents in his 2018 article "Equal Age for Age: The Growth, Death, and Rebirth of an Arizona Wine Industry, 1700–2000" in the *Journal of Arizona History*:

> *Despite rainy weather and limited publicity, the one-day event at the Santa Cruz County fairgrounds attracted some 1400 attendees. The following year it grew into a week-long event with over 6000 people. By 1986, the third festival included a wine-judging contest featuring some 25 different local wines.*

Since those early Sonoita days, Arizona wine events have proliferated, raising public awareness and introducing new generations to the wineries. In the southeastern region, these include the Off the Vine Arizona Wine Festival in Oro Valley, HarvestFest at Sonoita Vineyards, Sonoita Wine & Jazz Festival, St. Martin's Sonoita AVA New Release Festival, Kief-Joshua Vineyard's Magdalena Bash Harvest Festival, the Southeast Arizona Wine Growers Festival and the Willcox Wine Festival, which has been rated by Fodor's Travel as one of the top ten wine festivals in North America. In metro Phoenix and surrounding environs, visitors can celebrate Arizona wine at Grape Arizona, the Grand Wine Festival and

Chef Christopher Smith of Merkin Osteria and Sedona mayor Sandy Moriarty. *Becky Limberg.*

Grapes on the Grotto and as part of events such as the Devour Culinary Classic, Carefree Fine Art and Wine Festival and Tempe Festival of the Arts. Head north for the Spring Heritage Pecan and Wine Festival in Camp Verde, Wine in the Pines in Flagstaff, Verde Valley Wine Festival in Clarkdale, Wine and Dine in the Vines, Mother's Day Wine and Art Festival at Granite Creek Vineyards and Tilted Earth Festival at Page Springs Cellars.

"I think the wine industry is a fantastic economic engine for Arizona, all of Arizona," says Sedona mayor Sandy Moriarty, co-founder of the Sedona WineFest, one of the state's most popular festivals. Though Moriarty has been mayor since 2014, her support and appreciation for the Arizona wine industry stretches back further. Not only was she an early member of Jon Marcus's Echo Canyon wine club, but she has also lent a hand during harvest seasons, picking grapes at Echo Canyon and Page Springs Cellars. "I just think wine is endlessly interesting," she says. "All the nuances in how to make it, how it can be the same grape but taste very different from one winery to the next. There's always something to learn, and I've considered myself a lifelong learner."

In 2009, Moriarty co-founded the Sedona WineFest with Al Comello and Shondra Jepperson, which began with the Sedona Community Fair when her friends suggested adding a wine tent. "Because I knew all the winemakers at the time, they asked me if I would help organize that," says Moriarty, "so I said, 'Oh sure, I can do that.' And I put that first one together in seven weeks. One of those times when you're too dumb to know any better," she says with a chuckle. Nine wineries participated that first year.

Moriarty is proud of how the festival has grown, now with approximately twenty wineries and from 700 attendees the first year to 2,500 in 2018. "It's amazing," she says. "I really had not ever done anything like that. They quit doing the fair itself, and the WineFest became a standalone because it grew so much the second year. Now tourists come in annually just for this event." Mayor Moriarty is happy, but not surprised, by the ballooning interest and greater appreciation for Arizona's burgeoning wine industry. "The only way it could go was up," she says. "I always saw it as having so much potential as an economic driver for Arizona, and there's still plenty of room."

RAISING A GLASS TO THE FUTURE

With the farm-to-table ethos no longer a movement but a way of life, it's a natural progression that restaurants waving the banner of local sourcing should likewise celebrate the fruit of local vintners. If one were in Arizona and were to savor cheese from Crow's Dairy, freshly harvested Arizona pecans and crackers made with heritage grains from Hayden Mills, the perfect accompaniment should be a glass of wine produced from grapes grown, harvested, barreled and bottled in similar proximity, a premise that benefits those statewide and within the community. "It's so important to keep the money in our state," says sommelier T. Scott Stephens. "And it doesn't stop at the farmers' market. You have to do it all across the board, whether it's the dairy company, the farmer, the brewery, the distiller or the winery; we have to do it collectively." Peggy Fiandaca of LDV Winery agrees. "If you're concerned about what you eat and knowing where your food is coming from, you should do the same with your wine. There is a big difference between the ten-dollar box wine you're getting at the grocery store versus our eighteen-dollar bottle of Viognier. Our wines are so pure and clean compared to what it takes to put that wine in the store, and if you really care about what you're eating, you should be caring about what you're drinking too."

It's a momentous time for the Arizona wine industry. There's a tangible aura of being on the cusp of greatness. "It's a natural pattern," says Sam Pillsbury. "I mean, it happened in Australia. It happened in New Zealand. I've got people that I've known for years in New Zealand saying, 'What are you doing making wine in Arizona?' I tell them, 'You've got short memories. That's what someone was saying to you.'"

"As someone who has been selling Arizona wine for the better part of almost a decade now," says David Baird of Oddity Wine Collective, "this is the Wild West of winemaking. Nobody knows what we are doing, so we might as well do what we want. But we'll find what works. We are so fortunate in this day and age to be in this industry. There are a lot of bumps and a lot of legislation that we have to get through, but at the same time we get to be here in this experimental phase. I've never been a Boy Scout, but I'm pretty sure that we're blazing a couple of trails."

Wine, at its core, is an expression—an expression of the earth, the grapes and the hands and hearts that have coaxed *Vitis vinifera* into releasing its gifts. The history of wine is a woven tapestry of passion and perseverance, and in no place is that more evident than among the pioneering spirit of the

Arizona winemakers and the terroir they're tending. They are entrepreneurs, renegades and mavericks, overcoming preconceived notions and defining a region through trial and error, experimentation and fortitude.

"We have the most wonderful humans living in our backyard and producing this new industry," says T. Scott Stephens. "The reality is that it is the most special time ever to be a part of this. Not just the wineries, not just the people, not just the economy. It's things that are close to home and close to our heart. It's the whole package. When do you get a chance to be on the ground floor of a brand-new industry that is in its infancy but where the growth trajectory is limitless? I've tasted Malvasia from around the world, and I'll tell you, nothing tastes like our Malvasia. It's so aromatic and floral. It's beautiful. It's gorgeous. And look at the Gracianos and the Grenaches. Those are remarkable examples of what Arizona is capable of."

Mark Tarbell agrees. "Because of the integrity of those wines that are coming from those grapes, we are defining ourselves as a state in a unique way that isn't trying to chase the California profile. That's the best possible scenario because that is what is going to take Arizona to where it will have its own home, where it will have its own voice in the world of wine. And I think that's wonderful."

Cheers to Arizona!

T. Scott Stephens, Lisa Callaghan, Kent Callaghan, Katie Stephens and Todd Bostock at the 2019 Arizona Vignerons Alliance Symposium. *Becky Limberg.*

Bibliography

Ayers, Steve. "Featured Winery: Freitas Vineyard." *AZ Wine Lifestyle*, December 2011.

Beres, Mark. "Arizona Viticulture: Geography and Strong Wines." *AZ Wine Lifestyle*, March–June 2015, 79.

Berg, Erik. "Equal Age for Age: The Growth, Death, and Rebirth of an Arizona Wine Industry, 1700–2000." *Journal of Arizona History* (n.d.): 203–44.

Buhl, Al. "Perspectives on the Arizona Wine Industry, 1990–2013." *AZ Wine Lifestyle*, March 2013.

Camp Verde Bugle. "San Dominique Winery: A Celebration of Flavors and Tradition." October 29, 2001.

Dutt, Gordon, John R. Kuykendall, Eugene Mielke and T.W. McCreary. "A Toast to Arizona Wines!" *Arizona Land and People*. 1976, 1–5.

Glomski, Eric. "Frost in Arizona: What the Rest of the Country Doesn't Know." *AZ Wine Lifestyle*, September 2009.

Howard, William H. "In Search of Sedona History." William Howard Collection at the Sedona Historical Society, 1980.

Keenan, Maynard James. "Why Arizona?" *Phoenix New Times*, October 24, 2012.

Kino, Eusebio. *Kino's Historical Memoir of Pimería Alta: A Contemporary Account of the Beginnings of California, Sonora, and Arizona*. Cleveland, OH: Arthur H. Clark Company, 1919, 93.

Perez de Luxan, Diego. *Expedition into New Mexico Made by Antonio de Espejo, 1582–1583: As Revealed in the Journal of Diego Pérez de Luxán, a Member of the Party*. Translated by George Peter Hammond and Agapito Rey. Los Angeles: Quivira Society, 1929, 106.

Pillsbury, Sam. "Sam Pillsbury Spills on the Reason He Landed in Arizona, and Launches a Wine Column for Chow Bella." *Phoenix New Times*, April 25, 2013.

Webb, Robert W. "Grape Perspectives: 30 Years Too Soon." *AZ Wine Lifestyle*, September 2010.